Note:

At the time of writing, the reported apparitions of Our Lady at Medjugorje in Yugoslavia continue. Their authenticity is being investigated by a national commission named by the Bishops' Conference of Yugoslavia. This commission will report to the Holy See which makes the final decision. The authors of *A Medjugorje Retreat* submit to the Church's eventual judgment.

The messages of Our Lady quoted here have been given through one of the visionaries, Marija Pavlovic, for the parish of Medjugorje, and for the world. They are for all of us.

A Medjugorje Retreat

Robert Faricy, SJ and Lucy Rooney, SND

ALBA · HOUSE NEW · YORK

SOCIETY OF ST. PAUL, 2187 VICTORY BLVD., STATEN ISLAND, NEW YORK 10314 *for*

Leslie Wearne

Library of Congress Cataloging-in-Publication Data

Faricy, Robert L., 1926-
    A Medjugorje retreat / by Robert Faricy and Lucy Rooney.
        p.   cm.
    ISBN 0-8189-0558-1
    1. Mary, Blessed Virgin, Saint — Prayer-books and devotions —
English. 2. Mary, Blessed Virgin, Saint — Apparitions and miracles —
Yugoslavia — Medjugorje (Bosnia and Hercegovina) 3. Retreats.
4. Catholic Church — Prayer-books and devotions — English.
I. Rooney, Lucy. II. Title.
BT660.M44F37   1989
232.91'7'0949742 — dc20
                                                                89-32159
                                                                    CIP

Designed, printed and bound in the United States of
America by the Fathers and Brothers of the
Society of St. Paul, 2187 Victory Boulevard,
Staten Island, New York 10314, as part of their
communications apostolate.

Printing Information:

Current Printing - first digit   1   2   3   4   5   6   7   8   9   10   11   12

Year of Current Printing - first year shown
1989   1990   1991   1992   1993   1994   1995   1996

CONTENTS

Introduction: for an intensive retreat or
              for a retreat in everyday life ix

The story of Medjugorje 1

The first exercise: a foundational meditation 9

Part I:
Mary leads me to Jesus: the joyful mysteries

1. The angel announces the good news to Mary 15
2. Mary visits her cousin Elizabeth 18
3. Jesus, Mary, and Joseph in the stable 22
4. Mary and Joseph present Jesus in the temple 26
5. Mary and Joseph find Jesus in the temple 28

Part II: Conversion

1. Jesus forgives me 31
2. The prodigal son 35
3. Divine mercy 38

Part III: Faith

1. Jesus calls me to follow him 47
2. Jesus gives me his Spirit 53
3. Jesus heals me 56
4. Jesus is Lord 61
5. The Eucharist 67

Part IV:
The passion and death of Jesus:
the sorrowful mysteries and the stations of the cross

1. Jesus' agony in the garden 72
2. Jesus is scourged 73
3. Jesus is crowned with thorns 75
4. Stations one through ten: Jesus carries
   his cross 77
5. Stations eleven through fourteen:
   the crucifixion 90

Part V:
The peace of Christ: the glorious mysteries

1. Jesus has risen 98
2. The Ascension 102
3. Pentecost: receiving the Holy Spirit 111
4. The fourth and fifth glorious mysteries:
   the assumption of the Blessed Virgin Mary
   into heaven, and the crowning of Our Lady
   as Queen of Heaven 118
5. Final exercise: a contemplation for
   obtaining love 121

Master, where do you live?
"Come and see," he replied.
They came and saw . . .
and they stayed with him.
(John 1:38-39)

Let prayer take first place.
(Medjugorje,
message of November 1, 1984)

Mount Krizevac at dawn

For An Intensive Retreat or for A Retreat in Everyday Life

A spiritual retreat is exactly that, a retreating, withdrawal for a time from daily life, cares, work. Such a withdrawal or retreat can be made intensively for a period of time, several days for example, or even a month.

Or, you can make a retreat right within your regular everyday life, without taking any days off, by setting aside a special time for retreat prayer every day. A retreat made in everyday life, by taking forty-five minutes or an hour or a little longer every day to follow the retreat prayer exercises, has advantages. Since it does not involve a complete withdrawal from daily routine, it can help to integrate my relationship with the Lord into the daily relationships that make up my everyday life.

Why should I make a retreat? What is the point, the purpose, of making a retreat? To put more order and direction into my life. Perhaps to help me in making an important decision. But mainly to come closer to God, to deepen my relationship with the Lord.

This retreat book provides material for an intensive retreat of six or eight days; or less, if only some of the exercises are used. And, also, for making a retreat in everyday life.

For a six-day retreat or an eight-day retreat. If you use the book for an intensive six-day retreat, you can take four exercises, for an hour or so each, every day. This makes twenty-four prayer exercises, the number in the book. However, there is no need whatever to do all the prayer exercises, to finish the book. On the contrary, stay with an exercise until you have really finished with it. If you find the Lord in that exercise, stay there until you feel it is time to move on to the next exercise. Stay where you find facility in relating to the Lord. Then move on when you feel it is time. That way, you could spend more than one prayer-time, even three or four, on a single exercise. Stay where you find fruit.

Or you can use the book for an intensive eight-day retreat. You could plan tentatively to take three prayer exercises, for an hour or so each, every day. And then, near the end of the day, take the exercise where you found the most facility in relating to the Lord, and make that one, or a part of it again. However, the general rule holds: stay where you find fruit. No need to go on to the next exercise in your next prayer period if you really find the Lord where you are; stay with that exercise for one or more prayer times, until you think you have exhausted it and are ready to move to the next exercise.

For a retreat in everyday life. Many, perhaps most, will use this book to make a retreat in everyday life. If you have a regular prayer-time, a scheduled quiet time with the Lord every day, then you could make the retreat exercises during that time each day — say, for forty-five minutes or an hour or a little more. If your daily time for personal prayer is only a half hour, you may want to extend that time somewhat for the retreat.

If you make the retreat in everyday life, and if you do not already have a regular time for personal prayer, when and where should you pray? Where: choose a quiet place; it could be your own room, or a corner of the house, or in a church, or anywhere that you can be relatively quiet and not bothered. If you have small children in your care, or live in a dormitory and cannot get to church, or have a similar situation that seems to preclude finding a peaceful place and time to pray, you may need to use your imagination and make some adjustments. When: when you can, and when you can pray best. Early morning is good. For some, late at night works well. For others, two half-hour periods work best, maybe one at lunch break and one at night. Find your time and place, and try to stick to it. But do not be rigid. If you miss your prayer time for some reason, make it up later that day.

And remember: you do not necessarily have to take a new prayer exercise every day. You may find that, because you find a comparatively greater ease in being with the Lord in a given prayer exercise, you will want to repeat that exercise the following day. And maybe even for one or two days after that. If you do take one exercise each day, your retreat in daily life will take longer, and it could go on for quite a while.

For two or more people. You might want to share your retreat. If two or more of you make the retreat at the same time, whether a six- or eight-day retreat or a retreat in everyday life, you might want to get together on a regular basis to share with one another what the Lord is doing in your prayer, how you are getting along, what is happening in your retreat. You could share according to the three classic questions:

1. How is your prayer going?
2. What do you do when you pray?
3. How do you feel when you pray?

In an intensive retreat, you could share once a day. In a retreat in everyday life, you could share once or twice a week; or, if you live in the same house, briefly every day. Two persons can share, or three or four if they are all making the retreat.

You do not all have to be in the same place. One might go more slowly, repeating more exercises. But the point is to share and to support one another.

You can also pray together, out loud or silently, before or after you share. Advice is frequently not so useful. But praying together, ministering to one another through prayer, is a great help.

During your retreat, whether an intensive six- or eight-day retreat or an everyday life retreat, you should continue to take part in community worship and, if anything, increase it. Especially in an everyday life retreat, daily Mass, regular prayer meetings, church services, will fit right into the retreat and help it.

What is a Medjugorje retreat? Medjugorje, the Yugoslavian village where the Blessed Virgin Mary continues to appear, represents Mary, the mother of Jesus.

My relationship with Jesus is the number one priority in my life. But I can get badly out of focus, so Mary, our mother and God's mother, has, amazingly, returned to earth in our time; to straighten my vision, to call me to a loving one-to-one relationship with Jesus, God and Man.

To live in these times of her coming among us at Medjugorje is a great grace. So, in this Medjugorje retreat, we will fix our eyes on Jesus under the guidance of Mary who intercedes for us as she did at Cana (John 2:3).

The material for prayer. The retreat material, divided into twenty-four prayer exercises, combines two Christian traditions with the appearances and messages of the Blessed Virgin Mary in Yugoslavia. The outline of the twenty-four exercises follows the general dynamic of the *Spiritual Exercises* of St. Ignatius of Loyola, the sixteenth-century founder of the Jesuits. Within that framework, most of the proposals for prayer follow the fifteen mysteries of the rosary: joyful, sorrowful, glorious. All of this in the context of the appearances and messages of Our Lady at Medjugorje in Yugoslavia.

Each exercise begins with a "place" at Medjugorje, for example: in the parish church. The idea is to help you to make your retreat "at Medjugorje," even if you cannot go there to make the retreat. Each of the exercises situates you there. The photographs should help.

The rest of the material is to help you to pray. Read the material prayerfully; let the part or parts that strike you be food for your prayer. Then put it aside and begin your prayer. Repeat the prayer for "the grace I want," and enter into relationship with Mary or Jesus or both in terms of whatever struck you during your reading.

THE STORY OF MEDJUGORJE

"Dear children, I have chosen this parish in a special way, and I wish to lead it. I am guarding it in love" (March 1, 1984). Where is this special parish that Our Lady has chosen? Unexpectedly, it is in a Marxist state in the eastern bloc of European Communist-controlled countries; it is in the Federal People's Republic of Yugoslavia. Not unexpectedly, given Our Lady's preference, as shown in her choice of Lourdes, Fatima, Banneux, etc., it is a Nazareth-like rural community. Five villages make up the parish, having in all about five hundred and fifty families. The red-roofed whitewashed houses huddle together surrounded by fields of vines and tobacco. Each

family has a few tiny plots for its own vege-
tables. The older women pasture the family
cow and sheep or goats, spinning wool as they
go. Most of the field work is done laboriously by
hand. The produce is a state monopoly, so
brings little return. Women in babushkas, and
wearing full colorful skirts, trudge by with huge
bundles of twigs strapped to their backs for
kindling.

But already in 1981 the younger people
were changing. Blue denim jeans, often smug-
gled in from the West, were much sought after.
To lounge at the disco in the nearest town was
the favorite leisure activity. Though nominally
a Catholic community, religion was not a priority for most. All the vices of small-village life
were there in plenty. Our Lady had to say "I ask
you to stop slandering and pray for the unity of
the parish" (April 12, 1984), and "Honor the
wounds of my Son which he has received from
the sins of this parish" (March 22, 1984). A
volatile people, the older ones remember the
atrocities during the conflict between Catholics
(Croats) and Orthodox (Serbs) during and after
World War II.

Wednesday, June 24, 1981, had been a
blazingly hot day, but towards six in the evening
Mirjana Dragicevic and Ivanka Ivankovic left
the coolness of their stone houses to stroll along
the rough track past the hill Podbrdo. Sixteen

and fifteen years old, they were off to smoke a secret cigarette. These were normal young-sters, "not the best, but not the worst," as Vicka afterwards said. Ivanka was the first to notice something on the hillside above. "Look," she said, "there is Our Lady." "Oh, come on," an-swered Mirjana, "Our Lady wouldn't appear to us."

As they turned back to the village they met Milka on her way to bring the sheep home. So they accompanied her. Ivanka described what happened: "We went back, talking, and then we saw Our Lady. We knelt down and prayed there. The sheep went home. We chased them."

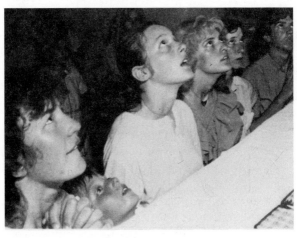

Vicka, Jakov, Ivanka, Mirjana, Marija and Ivan during an apparition, 1981

Meanwhile, Vicka Ivankovic, a seventeen-year-old, had been lying down, resting. She put on her slippers and went off to look for Mirjana and Ivanka. Vicka tells the story.

When I reached the road where they were, I saw they were waving and calling me to come. When I arrived up there, Mirjana said, "Look up there — Our Lady." I did not even look — did not have the time. I left my slippers and ran away barefoot. That was on the dirt and rock road. As I ran, I met Ivan Dragicevic and Ivan Ivankovic. They were picking apples and asked me if I wanted some. I said, "No" — and then, "Ivan, Our Lady! They say she is appearing up there. Come with me; I'm afraid." He, Ivan Dragicevic, sixteen years old, said, "What are you afraid of? Let's go."

I thought he wasn't afraid, but when we arrived and I turned to ask him: "Do you see anything?" he was already gone; I saw him running away. Ivan Ivankovic stayed. I asked him if he saw anything; he said he saw something completely white, moving. Milka, who was with us, said, "I see Our Lady."

Next day, as school was over for the sum-

4

mer, they had to return to their jobs in house and fields. But they agreed to meet and go again to Podbrdo in the early evening. Milka's mother, however, kept her busy, saying, "Let Marija go, that is enough."

Sixteen-year-old Marija Pavlovic, seeing Ivan Dragicevic, Vicka, Mirjana and Ivanka leaving for the hill, said to them: "I would like just to be there if you see Our Lady, even if I don't see her." They promised to call Marija and ten-year-old Jakov Colo. Ivan Ivankovic did not go that second day, thinking that it was childish to go to the hill for some vision or other. Several other children and two adults followed them. Vicka takes up the story:

> It was about six o'clock. Mirjana and I were walking together, talking. Ivanka was first, walking ahead of us. Suddenly she called: "Look! Our Lady!" It was still day, I was able to see her, the face, eyes, hair, gown, everything. We were down on the road and did not know what to do. I went to call Marija and Jakov. They came immediately. Our Lady called us to come up. Looking from the bottom of the hill, it seems close, but it is not. We were running at great speed. It was not like walking on the ground — we did not look for the pathway — we simply ran in the direction

where she was. It was like being pulled up into the air. I was afraid. We were there in five minutes, and though I was barefoot, no thorn hurt me.

The adults who were there confirm this. They were amazed at the speed and unable to keep up. Vicka continues:

When we were about two meters from Our Lady, we felt we were taken and dropped to our knees. Jakov knelt in a thorn bush. I thought, "He will be hurt," but he came out of it unharmed. Marija at first only saw something white but gradually it came clearer and she saw like the rest of us. Jakov said, "I see Our Lady."

So the group of six was formed, and to them Our Lady has since appeared daily. Mirjana's visions ceased on December 25, 1982, and Ivanka's on May 6, 1985. The other four continue.

Our Lady revealed her purpose on the third evening when she said, in response to the question "Why have you come?" "I want to be with you; to convert and to reconcile everyone." She described herself as the Queen of Peace.

During these years, Our Lady has been forming the people of the parish in their daily

Christian lives, by a series of messages, given through Marija Pavlovic. At her request, several prayer groups of young people have been established, and these she guides by messages, locutions or visions. To all of them, her most often repeated call is to prayer: "Pray, pray, pray!" "Prayer is your life" (September 25, 1987).

Statue of the risen Jesus outside the church at Medjugorje

THE FIRST EXERCISE:
A FOUNDATIONAL MEDITATION

A prayer before starting. Lord Jesus, thank you that I can spend this retreat time with you. I ask you, Jesus, to be my retreat director. I open my heart so that you may speak to me and guide me.

Note. Jesus is calling me to be with him. He is giving me a chance to start over, to put order into my life. He wants my life to be centered on him. He wants to start over with me.

Let him do it all. It is not my effort that matters, but my acceptance. My part is to listen, to spend time with him, so that I may give him a chance to speak. He *will* speak to me in my heart. Sometimes we pray, and hope God hears us, but really prayer is God speaking to us. He says:

> Listen; listen to me!
> Pay attention!
> Come to me.
> Listen, so that your soul may live.
>> (Isaiah 55:2b-3).

Foundational meditation. The foundation of the retreat, as of my life, is Jesus.

Kneel before Our Blessed Lady as the six young visionaries do. They see her; she is just as truly present to you. "Tell them to believe as if they see," she said. And here is what Mary said at Medjugorje regarding the purpose of your life.

> Dear children, I want each one of you to start living in God's love. I am your mother, and on this account desire to lead each one of you to holiness in all its completeness. I want every one of you to be both happy here on earth, and then with me in heaven. This, dear children, is my purpose in coming here, as well as my desire (May 25, 1987).

In your own words, ask Mary to lead you now to Jesus, to help you to pray to Jesus and to understand better the meaning and purpose of your life.

The grace I want. To know Jesus, to know his love for me, and to better understand in the light of his love the meaning and purpose of my life.

My relationship with Jesus is the center of my life. But he is God; how can I speak of having a personal, loving relationship with someone who is God? I can, because the invitation comes from his side:

> The Lord has appeared to us from afar, saying, "I have loved you with an everlasting love; I have drawn you with loving kindness" (Jeremiah 31:3).
> Greater love has no one than this, that one lay down his life for his friends. You are my friends (John 15:13).

The meaning of my life. What is the meaning of my life? What was God's purpose in lovingly creating *me* — not anyone else he could have made, but the me he thought up, designed, and brought into existence with great joy?

11

When the morning stars sang together and all the sons of God shouted for joy (Job 38:7).

The catechism tells us that the meaning of my life is "to know, love, and serve God in this world, and to be happy with him in the next." Yes, but God had an ultimate personal purpose for my life when he "created me in Christ Jesus."

For we are his workmanship, created in Christ Jesus (Ephesians 2:10).

Let him show me now during my prayer time, in the light of his love, the reason I exist, his personal call to *me*.

Certainly he is calling me to a personal relationship that is close, intimate. In this retreat Jesus wants to help me so that all my other relationships and activities will be organized and ordered from that central relationship. Jesus wants to come into my life in greater strength and greater power.

Here is a prayer to Jesus; say it slowly, looking at Jesus with the eyes of faith.

Lord Jesus, thank you for designing me, for creating me, for loving me, for dying

for me. I need to know you, Lord Jesus,
the One who loves me so much. I want to
walk always with you. I want to abide in
you as you in me. Speak to me, Jesus; show
me your face.

Scripture texts which may help your prayer:
Ephesians 1:3-23; Psalm 139:1-18.

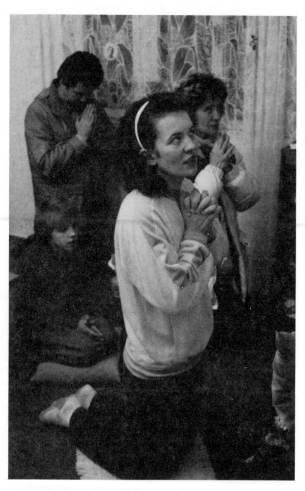

The Blessed Virgin appears to Vicka at her home

Mary Leads Me To Jesus: The Joyful Mysteries

1. *The angel announces the good news to Mary*

  Place. The main room in the home of Vicka Ivankovic, one of the young people who see the Blessed Virgin. For several years Vicka has been ill with frequent headaches and other sufferings. After her illness began, she stopped going with the other visionaries to meet Our Lady every evening. Instead, Mary began to come to Vicka in the living room of her family's house in the village of Bijakovici, near Medjugorje village and part of the same parish.

The angel Gabriel came to Mary in much the same setting: in a quiet village lost in the hills far from any major city. A village where the people lived simply and poorly, worked hard, and spoke with a heavy local accent. The angel came to an uneducated young woman with good news for the world if she said "Yes."

And she did. She became the mother of Jesus, and so the mother of our salvation, the mother of grace, the mother of each of us.

Message from Our Lady

I invite each one of you to make an option in favor of complete abandonment to me. Only thus will I in turn be enabled to offer you to God. You are aware, dear children, that I love you immensely and want each of you to belong to me. However, God has given each of you free will. I respect it with the greatest love, and humbly submit to your power of free choice (November 25, 1987).

Scripture text

The angel Gabriel was sent from God to a city of Galilee named Nazareth, to a virgin

16

engaged to a man named Joseph, of the house of David. The virgin's name was Mary.

The angel came to her and said, "Hail, you who are full of grace; the Lord is with you. Blessed are you among women." What he said disturbed her greatly, and she puzzled over what kind of greeting this could be.

And the angel said to her, "Fear not, Mary. You have found favor with God. Behold, you will conceive in your womb and give birth to a son, and you will call him Jesus. He will be great, and will be called Son of the Most High. God will give him the throne of David his ancestor. He will reign over the house of Jacob forever, and his kingdom will never end."

Then Mary said to the angel, "How can this happen, because I am a virgin?" The angel answered her, "The Holy Spirit will come upon you, and the power of the Most High will cover you with its shadow. And therefore the child will be holy and will be called the Son of God. . . ."

Mary said, "Behold the handmaid of the Lord. Let what you have said be done to me" (Luke 1:26-38).

Prayer for the grace I want. Mary, my mother, pray with me now and for me, for the grace to

17

know Jesus better so that I can love him more and follow him more closely. Help me to enter into the mystery of the Annunciation and of the Incarnation — God becomes human in your womb.

Lord Jesus, I want to know you better, to love you more, and to follow you more closely. Help me to know you better through love, especially through your love for me that made you become human so as to save me. Help me to say "Yes" to you, now and always, in everything, the way Mary said "Yes" to God's plan. Amen.

During your prayer time. Your prayer might take the form more of a "thinking about," a kind of meditation or consideration of the meaning of God's becoming human through the Blessed Virgin Mary. Or it could be a prayerful talking to or being with Mary, or with Jesus. Or with both, together or one after the other. Pray the way you feel led to pray, the way that seems to suit you best now, however you are most at ease praying.

2.   *Mary visits her cousin Elizabeth*

Place. Podbrdo hill, where Our Lady appeared to the six young people in the beginning of her daily visits to the Medjugorje area. The hill of Podbrdo rises behind the tiny village of Bijakovici where all six of the young people lived in the summer of 1981. Mirjana had begun to spend her summer vacation there, and the other five — Ivanka, Vicka, Ivan, Marija, and Jakov — all live there. The houses of Vicka, Marija, and Ivan stand at the foot of Podbrdo on the first slope of the hill that goes up from the road through the village.

Mary came to this place, lost in the hills of Bosnia-Herzegovina, just as she went after the Annunciation to visit her cousin Elizabeth in the hill country of Galilee. On her visit to Elizabeth, Mary carried the as yet unborn Jesus. Mary always brings Jesus, and she always brings us to Jesus. Meeting Our Lady always means meeting Jesus.

Message from Our Lady

> Rejoice with me! My heart is rejoicing in Jesus today; I want to give him to you. I am praying for each one of you and am presenting you to God. In this way he will manifest himself to you (December 25, 1987).

Scripture text

> At that time Mary left and quickly went into the hill country to a town of Judah.

She went to the house of Zechariah and greeted Elizabeth. When Elizabeth heard Mary's greeting, her baby leaped in her womb, and Elizabeth was filled with the Holy Spirit. She spoke out with a loud voice and said, "Blessed are you among women, and blessed is the fruit of your womb. And how is it that my Lord's mother should come to me? The instant the sound of your greeting came to my ears, the baby leaped for joy in my womb. And blessed is she who believed in the fulfillment of the Lord's promise."

And Mary said:

"My soul proclaims the greatness of the Lord,

my spirit rejoices in God my Savior,

for he has looked with favor on his lowly servant.

From this day all generations will call me blessed;

the Almighty has done great things for me,

and holy is his Name.

He has mercy on those who fear him

in every generation.

He has shown the strength of his arm,

he has scattered the proud in their conceit.

He has cast down the mighty from their thrones,

and has lifted up the lowly.
He has filled the hungry with good things,
and the rich he has sent away empty.
He has come to the help of his servant
    Israel
for he has remembered his promise of
    mercy,
the promise he made to our fathers,
to Abraham and his children for ever."

(Luke 1:39-55)

Prayer for the grace I want. Ask Our Lady to come to you now, in your prayer, to teach you to pray and to live, to guide your prayer and your life, and to bring Jesus to you — and to bring you to him.

During your prayer time. Go to Mary. Let her come to visit you the way she visited her cousin Elizabeth, the way she visits the young people every day in Medjugorje. Ask her to come to you. Even if you do not feel or in any way sense her presence, know that she is present to you, your mother. Be with her, in that presence — perhaps completely unfelt, perhaps entirely in the dark.

Then see how she helps you to pray, how she guides your prayer. Talk to her. Ask her to teach you and to help you to pray. Ask her to guide you in your prayer and in your life.

You might want to say the Magnificat, "My soul proclaims the greatness of God . . . ," together with her, a line at a time, very slowly. Say it together with Our Lady. Let each word, line, thought, sink in and become a part of you.

3. *Jesus, Mary, and Joseph in the stable*

Place. Inside the church of St. James. In front of you is the main altar. On your left, off the sanctuary, is the sacristy where the priests vest for the concelebrated Masses that take place during the day in various languages, and in the evening, after the appearance of the Blessed Virgin Mary, in Croatian.

The appearances of Our Lady to the young people moved from the hill of Podbrdo to the secondary sacristy room, on your right, just off the altar, in 1981 when the local communist government objected to a religious gathering outside a church building. Later, when the local bishop objected to Our Lady's appearing in church, they moved to the parish house where the Franciscan priests live. Finally, when the bishop insisted that the young people not have any special place to meet Our Lady, but that they just go to church like everyone else, the appearances moved back to the church. Usually the young people, or one or two of them, go to the church balcony, behind you as you face the altar, and Mary comes to them there before the evening rosary and Mass.

During the Christmas season, an elaborate Nativity scene, a "crib," stands just in front of the main altar. This Christmas scene in the church helps those who pray there to enter into the mystery of Jesus' birth and infancy, the mystery of God, "born of a woman" (Galatians 4:4), coming among us as a baby, as Savior, as Redeemer, as Counselor, as Wonderful.

The church of St. James, 1982. Fathers Vlasic, Forrest and Faricy

Message from Our Lady

I invite you to give glory to Jesus together with me. I will give him to you in a special way on that day [of his nativity], and I invite you on that day to give glory and praise with me to Jesus at his birth (December 12, 1985).

Scripture text

And she brought forth her firstborn, and wrapped him in swaddling clothes, and laid him in a manger because there was no room for them in the inn.

And there were in the same region shepherds in the fields keeping watch by night over their flocks. Suddenly an angel of the Lord appeared to them and the glory of the Lord shone around them. They were terrified. But the angel said to them, "Do not be afraid; listen to me; I bring you good news of great joy. Today, to you, in the city of David, a Savior is born, Christ the Lord. And here is a sign for you: you will find the baby wrapped in swaddling clothes and lying in a manger."

Then suddenly there was with the angel a multitude of the army of heaven praising God and saying, "Glory to God in the highest, and on earth peace and good will to all."

When the angels had left and gone back to heaven, the shepherds said to one another, "Let us go now to Bethlehem and see what has happened, what God has made known to us." And they went quickly, and found Mary and Joseph, and the baby lying in a manger.

(Luke 2:7-16)

Prayer for the grace I want. Mary, my mother, help me to know Jesus better so that I can love him more and follow him more closely. Help me to enter into the mystery of the Nativity. Let me be with you and Joseph and the shepherds, looking at Jesus with reverence and love.

Jesus, I come to you with the Blessed Virgin Mary, your mother and mine. I ask you for the grace to enter into the mystery of the first Christmas so that I can know you better, love you more, and follow you more closely. Amen.

During your prayer time. Go right to Jesus. Let Mary take you to him. And let Jesus draw you into his heart, into his memory of the first Christmas. Let him take you into that memory that he has in his heart. Let Jesus make you present at the scene: Mary and Joseph in the stable with the baby Jesus.

Just stay there and see what happens, how the Lord leads your prayer. Remain peaceful and quiet.

4.   *Mary and Joseph present Jesus in the temple*

Place. Inside the parish church. This church is special to the Blessed Virgin Mary because it is the church of the parish she has chosen for herself, to guide it, to encourage it, and to mother it spiritually. It is the church of a group of poor village people whom Mary guides in a special way and for whom she prays in a special way.

You are there now, at least in your imagination, in that church, and — in spirit — part of that parish. Let yourself be mothered by Mary.

Message from Our Lady

In a particular way I invite you at this time to pray to be able to live the experience of the joy of the meeting with the newborn Jesus. I wish to guide you and to show you the joy to which I want to lead each one of you. Therefore, dear children, pray, and abandon yourselves totally to me (December 11, 1986).

> . . . they took him up to Jerusalem to present him to the Lord, as it is written in the law of the Lord, "Every firstborn male shall be called holy to the Lord," and also to offer a sacrifice according to what is said in the law of the Lord, a pair of turtledoves or two young pigeons (Luke 1:23-24).

Prayer for the grace I want. Ask Our Lady to pray for you and with you, to present you to Jesus just as she presented Jesus to the Father. Ask especially for the grace to know Jesus better so as to love him more and follow him more closely.

During your prayer time. Go to Mary; ask her to take you to Jesus, and with Jesus to the Father. Say to Mary, and to Jesus, and to the Father, what is in your heart.

You might want to spend some time praying about the other things that took place in the temple at the time of the presentation: Simeon's prayer and prophecy (Luke 2:25-35), and the praise and prophecy of Anna (Luke 2:36-38). You might want to reflect on these, and go over them with Mary or Jesus or both.

5. *Mary and Joseph find Jesus in the temple*

Place. The parish church of St. James.

Message from Our Lady

> Dear children, in these days the Father offers particular graces to all those who open their hearts. I bless you, and desire that you too, dear children, know these graces, and place all at God's disposal, so that God may be glorified through you. I follow your footsteps attentively (December 25, 1986).

Scripture text

> When they were on the way home after the feast, the boy Jesus stayed behind in Jerusalem without his parents knowing about it. . . . After three days they found him in the temple, sitting among the doctors, listening to them and asking them questions. He astonished everyone who heard him with his intelligence and his answers.
>
> They were astounded when they saw him, and his mother said to him, "Child, why have you done this to us? Your father and I have been very worried looking for you."

Jesus said to them, "Why were you looking for me? Didn't you know that I have to be involved in the things of my Father?" But they did not understand what he meant (Luke 2:41-50).

Prayer for the grace I want. Mary, help me to know Jesus better. You did not understand him

Crowds around the Church of St. James

completely even though you have always known him better than any other human being. Pray for me and with me now that I can know him better and so love him more and follow him more closely.

Jesus, teach me to know you better so that I can love you more and follow you more closely.

During your prayer time. You might want to talk to Mary or to consider with her how she felt: her anguish about losing Jesus, and then her joy at finding him, and her lack of understanding of what he meant by his words to her in the temple. You might want to talk to Jesus and to think over in his loving presence how he felt and what he meant by what he said to Joseph and Mary when they found him in the temple.

You could, also, just go to Jesus and let him draw you into his presence, into his love, into his heart and his memory of what happened. Let him show you the meaning of the scripture text. The understanding Jesus will give you may not be able to be put into words or clear ideas. But he will help you to know him better by revealing to you in some way, perhaps in a real darkness of faith, who he is for you.

PART II

Conversion

Note on conversion. Many of Our Lady's messages at Medjugorje call us to conversion. Conversion means turning, turning *from* my sins and my sinfulness and my coldness toward the Lord, and turning *to* him in sorrow for my sins, and accepting his forgiveness and mercy.

Conversion is not just a one-time event. Conversion is a process. I am a sinner. I need continuous conversion.

The second part of the retreat helps me to turn from sin and to the Lord. And to open my heart to his compassionate and healing forgiveness.

1. *Jesus forgives me*

Place. At the foot of the cross on Mount Krizevac. Our Lady has frequently appeared here.

Message from Our Lady

> I ask you to offer up to the Lord your whole past, all the evil that has accumulated in your hearts. I want each of you to be happy, but sin prevents this (February 25, 1987).

Prayer for the grace I want. Lord Jesus, I have sinned against your love. I ask you for real sorrow, that comes from love, and that will lead me to accept your forgiveness, and change my life.

Reflection: what is sin? A consciousness of sin in my life can be on several levels:

(a) I break God's law. Even a dog knows when it has done wrong, and will hang its tail, waiting for a cuff. But it has no sense of "sin" and of "guilt." Its "guilt" is just the fear of the displeasure of its master. This kind of sorrow for sin — that I have broken God's law — leads only to remorse, fear of punishment, fear of damnation.

(b) Sin hurts me. I suffer the consequences that I bring on myself now: loss of self-worth, illness, social consequences. This sorrow leads to regret: I have failed; I am not a true, straight person.

32

(c) Sin seen in the light of God's love:

> In this the love of God was made manifest among us, that God sent his only Son into the world . . . to be the expiation for our sins (1 John 4:9-10).

Here I clearly see my sin as a refusal of love, a rejection of his love. Jesus loves me *totally* and *unconditionally*. But when I sin, I am saying to him: "No thanks, not today, because I want to do this thing that I know is wrong. I really prefer myself to you." If only I knew, realized, the love of God and what it is I am rejecting, whom I am grieving by refusing to accept and return love. But:

> Love is strong as death
> its jealousy unyielding as the grave.
> It burns like a blazing fire,
> like a mighty flame.
> Many waters cannot quench love;
> rivers cannot wash it away.
>
> (Song of Songs 8:6)

> This is love: not that we loved God, but that he loved us, and sent his Son as an atoning sacrifice for our sins (1 John 4:10).

Reflection: sin in my life. I need to know my sinfulness. Jesus, I ask you to show me my sin.

Show me where I am refusing your love, letting you down. Jesus, what do you reproach in me?

To face sin in our lives we need to stand in God's love. Do not dig around; just fix your eyes on Jesus crucified, and let him show you where you are refusing love. When he shows you some area, be honest. At the moment of temptation we rationalize (for example, "I'm really being dishonest about this money, but life owes it to me anyway").

Behind these sins are their roots — basic sinful tendencies. Let Jesus show you these, for example, sloth, self-protection, vanity, inordinate attachments — to my job or to money, to people, to an excessive need for esteem. If my sin is in the area of love, I need to realize that I cannot love too much, but that I can love in a way that is not in the Lord, possessively, selfishly. Love always leaves a person free. Jesus leaves me free.

During your prayer time. One way to pray is to go through your life in stages, seeing where you have refused love, seeing your disordered ways of loving things, self, others. But your eyes should be more on Jesus than on self. Listen to him.

Prayer for the grace I want. Lord Jesus, I ask you to show me my sinfulness, where I have failed you by rejecting your love. Touch my

heart so that true sorrow may lead me to repent
and change.

Scripture texts that may be helpful:
Psalm 51; Galatians 5:15-16;
Ephesians 2:1-10.

2. *The prodigal son*

Place. At the foot of the cross on Mount
Krizevac, with Mary.

Message from Our Lady

Dear children, I, your mother, love you,
and wish to urge you to prayer. I am tire-
less, dear children, and I call you even
when you are far away from my heart. I
feel pain for everyone who has gone a-
stray. But I am a mother, and I forgive
easily; and I rejoice over every child who
comes back to me (November 14, 1985).

Scripture text

Jesus said, "I tell you, there is joy before
the angels of God over one sinner repent-
ing" (Luke 15:10).

Reflection: the prodigal father. (Read Luke 15:11-32).

The parable of the prodigal son could just as well be called "the prodigal father." At least the younger son, profligate though he was, was more like his father: generous, willing to share and give, than the rigid elder son. The father was prodigal in giving, forgiving, and loving. He forgave freely, and, running, threw his arms around his lost son. He had been straining his eyes while the boy was "a long way off." The son was a long way off from true sorrow and repentance. He was in despair because he had made such a mess of his life — hungry, deserted by fair-weather friends, brought down to the level of pigs. His human dignity was gone because of his foolishness and sin.

He returned to his father, thinking he was coming home in repentance, but actually he was intending to bargain: "Father, I have sinned . . . make me one of your servants." In other words, "I will make it up to you, I will earn my way."

But his father's attitude changed all that. The loving, persevering waiting, the forgetting of personal dignity to pick up his robes and run, the embrace, the unquestioning restoration, brought the son to true repentance: "Father I have sinned . . . I am not worthy to be called your son."

My repentance must not be an attempt to bargain, to restore myself. I can only humbly say that I lack even true sorrow, and ask for the gift, which is a real grace, of accepting the Lord's loving forgiveness which enables me humbly but happily to start over; of letting the Lord put order in my life, transform my life. Then I can join in the music and dancing at the party for forgiven sinners.

> There will be more joy in heaven over one sinner who repents than over ninety-nine righteous persons who need no repentance (Luke 15:7).

Prayer. Lord Jesus, I am sorry for my sins. I repent. And, relying on your grace, and in your name, Jesus, I renounce my sins, especially [name your main sins and sinful tendencies]. I renounce the devil and his works. I renounce my selfishness, my pride, and the excessive love of pleasure. [Renounce anything which you see is an obstacle between you and God, such as fear, anger, depression, anxiety, irritability.] Lead me, Jesus, to the Father. Help me to accept his mercy and love.

During the hour of prayer, repent, and accept the mercy and love which Jesus and the Father extend to you.

scripture texts that may be helpful:
> Jeremiah 31:3-4; Hosea 11:3-4;
> Psalm 51 "Have mercy . . .";
> Galatians 5:15-26; Ephesians 2:1-10.

3. *Divine mercy*

Place. Mount Krizevac, at the foot of the cross. In your imagination, see the blood and water pouring from Jesus' heart.

Message from Our Lady

> Pray in a special way before the cross; many graces come from the cross.
>> (September 12, 1985)

> Jesus gives you special gifts from the cross. Accept them and live them.
>> (February 20, 1986)

Scripture text

> Jesus said, "I tell you, there will be more joy in heaven over one sinner repenting than over ninety-nine just people who have no need of repentance" (Luke 15:7).

Prayer for the grace I want. Jesus, I need to know you. Please show yourself to me as Mercy made human.

Reflection: God's mercy. This retreat is never just an exercise of the mind. Each prayer time is an actual meeting with the Lord, face to face. I meet Jesus now as the mercy of God incarnate.

Mercy is, by definition, unearned, undeserved. God showed his mercy to me when he freely gave his only and beloved Son up to an atrocious death, on my behalf.

> He saved us not because of the righteous things we had done, but because of his mercy (Titus 3:5).

At the foot of the cross

Original sin has left me morally frail from the beginning of my life. My actual sins have compounded my inclination to sin. I could despair of myself, if ever I have got into a morass of sin and sinful living, or even into an addictive habit of sin. I can even despair of my ability to respond to the grace of God. I am so often "converted," only to fall again. Did the prodigal son persevere — did he go back to his old friends, to his wastrel life? If he did would his father take him back a second, a third time? In my frailty, the scriptures give me the answer: keep coming back to Jesus, because

> His mercy never fails.
> It is new every morning.
> Great is your faithfulness.
> I say to myself:
> The Lord is my portion.
> Therefore I will wait for him.
> (Lamentations 3:22-24)

Nothing pleases God more than being merciful to me and forgiving me.

You *delight* to show mercy (Micah 7:18).

Mercy is compassion. *Com*passion suffers with. God knows what is in me; he has known me from before I was formed in my mother's womb, nothing is hidden from him (cf. Psalm

139:13ff). He knows ahead of time what I will do — yet he does not abandon me, give me up, or say "It is useless to lay down my life for such a one." No:

> God loved us with so much love that he was generous with his mercy: when we were dead through our sins, he brought us to life with Christ (Ephesians 2:4).

What does he do? Each time I have come back to him, he has forgiven me. He did not say "I forgive you, but how could you do such a thing?" No:

> He threw all my sins behind his back.
> (Isaiah 38:17)

They are gone. If I were to ask him, he would not know of them.

> In Christ, God was reconciling the world to himself, not counting their sins against them (2 Corinthians 5:19).

My sins have been taken away. Now I am face to face with Jesus, with our Father, open to receive mercy. I just open my heart. The prophet Hosea assured us:

He will come to us like the winter rains and like the spring rains (Hosea 6:3).

Rains in the land Jesus and Hosea knew are no gentle showers, but torrential deluges, cascading down from the skies. God pours out his compassionate mercy on my sins like those rains. Hosea continued God's tender lament over us sinners:

What shall I do with you? Your love is like the early dew that disappears (Hosea 6:4).

Yes, Jesus, I know I am like that. I know I am a fragile vessel holding such a treasure (cf. 2 Corinthians 4:7). I am easily broken. But Jesus, I come back to you each time. I am sitting in the rain of your mercy. Soak each hard, unfruitful area of my life. Wash away my sin; refresh me, bring new life. Make a new springtime in my life.

Jesus responds:
I have dispelled your faults like a cloud,
your sins like a mist.
Come back to me, for I have redeemed you.
(Isaiah 44:22)

Prayer. God of mercy, I am here, holding up my life to the abundant rain of your mercy. Jesus, I do not want to put any barriers between my sins and your mercy — putting umbrellas up to keep your mercy out of sinful areas — sins to which I am still attached. Jesus, I expose my whole life to your compassionate mercy.

During your prayer time. I need not be afraid to "look my sins in the face," as long as my eyes are at the same time on Jesus' love for me, and his merciful forgiveness. He loves me, partly, indeed, because of my sins, as a handicapped child in a family is specially loved.

Scripture texts if you need them.
Luke 15; Psalm 51.

PART III

Faith

Note on faith. The Blessed Virgin Mary at Medjugorje has frequently called us to greater faith. She prays for greater faith for each of us, and I can pray with her to Jesus, "Lord, increase my faith!"

What is faith? Faith means not only believing the truths that God has revealed. It includes that, but faith goes beyond agreeing to the truth of Christianity. Faith means believing in Jesus Christ, adhering to him, hanging on to him. And in him is contained all truth; he is the Truth as well as the Way and the Life.

Faith means accepting Jesus' personal call to a close union with him, to discipleship, to friendship, to follow him wholeheartedly. And faith is a gift.

This third part of the retreat is intended especially to help growth in faith. "Lord, increase my faith."

Podbrdo; site of the first apparitions

1. *Jesus calls me to follow him*

Place. Podbrdo. Kneel with the six young people before Our Lady. Listen as she speaks to you.

Message from Our Lady

I desire that you come to understand that God has chosen each one of you, so that he may be able to use you in his great plan for the salvation of all mankind. It is beyond your comprehension how great your role is in God's designs. Therefore you must pray, dear children, so that in so doing, you may be enabled to grasp what God plans to achieve through you. I am with you in order that God's plan may be brought about in all its fullness.

(January 25, 1987)

Scripture text

He called to him those he wanted, and they came to him (Matthew 13:13).

Reflection: Jesus chooses. Imagine yourself as part of that crowd sitting around Jesus on the hillside, as you are sitting now. He starts calling out the names of those whom he chooses. You catch your breath: will he call my name?

47

I have called you by name, you are mine.
(Isaiah 43:1)

Yes, he called your name when he dreamed you
up before creation began.

> Before the world was made, he [the
> Father] chose us, chose us in Christ.
> (Ephesians 1:4)

He has renewed his call throughout your life.

> God never takes back his gifts or revokes
> his choice (Romans 11:29).

Now in this retreat he is speaking to you again,
choosing and calling you to follow him. Your
making this retreat can be only his initiative, his
call, because the initiative is always his:

> You did not choose me; no, I chose you.
> (John 15:16)

So say "Yes" to Jesus' choice and call.

Reflection: the disciple. What does a disciple
do? He goes to the school of his master. He lets
himself be taught, he learns the ways of his
master, listens to his teaching, has his eyes on
the master. That is our part, to be face to face
with Jesus. Prayer is Jesus' school.

Each morning he wakes me to hear, to listen, like a disciple (Isaiah 50:4).

Prayer and scripture are where I find Jesus. You cannot get to know a person without spending time with that person.

> Give your undivided attention to the Lord.
> (1 Corinthians 7:35)

Watch Jesus in the gospels; get to know his ways, the things that are important to him. When you love a person, that person's voice, their gestures, are recognizable anywhere, and touch the heart. The two disciples on the road to Emmaus recognized Jesus as he broke bread. They would not have been at the last supper, not being apostles, so it was not the Eucharist they recognized. There must have been a way Jesus held and broke bread, that they knew. All his life he must have had a reverence for bread, since he selected it: "I am the bread of life"; "This is my body." So when "he took bread and blessed and broke it, and gave it to them, their eyes were opened, and they recognized him." Get to know Jesus in love.

John, when he was very old, reflecting on his memories of Jesus, writes of knowledge-in-love:

49

That which we have heard, and we have seen with our own eyes, that we have watched, and touched with our hands; the Word (1 John 1:1).

Reflection: sent out. When the disciple has spent time face to face with his teacher, his master, then he goes out, side by side with him. Chosen, called, sent. The master is still with the disciple in the work he gives him to do.

He has given me a disciple's tongue to know the word that sustains the weary.
(Isaiah 50:4)

The Samaritan woman (John 4) was the one Jesus chose out of all the Samaritans. She, as Jesus observed, had had five husbands, and the man she was currently living with was not her husband. But Jesus chose her.

He called us not because of anything we ourselves have done, but for his own purpose and by his own grace.
(2 Timothy 1:9)

Those who are common and contemptible are the ones God has chosen.
(1 Corinthians 1:28)

The woman looks at Jesus, listens to him, asks questions (she is a disciple in his school). Then she goes and tells her neighbors. They come to see for themselves. She is called, chosen, sent. The result is:

> The Samaritans of that town had believed on the strength of the woman's testimony . . . Now they said to the woman: "We no longer believe because of what you told us; we have heard him ourselves and we know that he really is the savior of the world" (John 4:19, 42)

Reflection: what is asked of a disciple? The disciple is asked for fidelity — for a single heart.

> No one can serve two masters: he will either . . . treat the first with respect, and the second with scorn (Matthew 6:24).

I cannot serve myself, choose myself, if I am to be a disciple. This is difficult, and I must face it if I want to answer Jesus' call. The word "discipline" goes along with the word "disciple."

> If anyone comes to me and does not hate . . . even his own life, he cannot be my disciple (Luke 14:26).

My motive in all I do can only be the one Jesus had:

> I have come from heaven not to do my own will, but to do the will of the one who sent me (John 6:38).

Fidelity in doing what I discern the Lord wants, begins in the little things of my day. That way, I will be faithful in the bigger things when they turn up.

> Catch the foxes, the little foxes that make havoc of the vineyards.
>
> (Song of Songs 2:15)

In my daily life I have to watch out for the "little foxes," the little things where I choose myself, not Jesus, for they can make havoc of my life with him.

Jesus said to the Samaritan woman, "If only you knew what God is offering you" (John 4:10). If, if only! I do not want, when I come to die, to say, "If only I had known what God was offering me." I want to give him my whole heart, my whole life, my whole will, right now in my prayer, and then each day, keeping nothing back, keeping no area of my life for myself. Ask for the strong grace to do this, so as to be one of

> . . . his followers, the called, the chosen, the faithful (Revelation 17:14).

Prayer. Lord Jesus, I come to you with Mary, your mother and my mother too. I offer myself to you to be your follower, your disciple. Thank you for inviting me to join you, to be with you, to follow you. I accept you totally as my Lord and my God. I give myself to you; help me to be generous in giving myself to you. Amen.

Scripture readings: John 4:5-42;
                        Matthew 4:18-22;
                        Matthew 9:9-13.

2. *Jesus gives me his Spirit*

Place. The hill of Podbrdo at the spot where Our Lady first appeared.

Message from Our Lady

> Turn your hearts to prayer and ask that the Holy Spirit be poured upon you.
> (May 9, 1985)

Scripture text

> Then Jesus appeared. He came from Galilee to the Jordan to be baptized by

John. John forbade him, saying, "I need to be baptized by you, and you come to me?" Jesus answered him, "Let it be this way for now so that we can fulfill all righteousness." Then John gave in to him.

When Jesus was baptized, he came up out of the water, and suddenly the heavens opened, and he saw the Spirit of God descending like a dove, coming upon him. And a voice from heaven spoke: "This is my beloved Son, in whom I am well pleased" (Matthew 3:13-17).

Prayer for the grace I want. I pray to open my heart to Jesus and to receive a greater outpouring of his Holy Spirit.

Reflection: the baptism of Jesus. At his baptism by John, Jesus received a new fullness of the Holy Spirit. John baptizes Jesus in the water of the Jordan River, but the Father baptizes Jesus in the Holy Spirit. This "baptism in the Holy Spirit" is an anointing by the Father of Jesus in the Spirit. Jesus, anointed with the Holy Spirit, can now begin his apostolic life, his mission as the Messiah, as the "Christ" (which means: the "anointed").

When he receives the Holy Spirit, Jesus receives power for his life. He is, anew, in a new and important way, empowered in and by the

Spirit. The Holy Spirit empowers because he is the powerful Love of the Father and Jesus.

Jesus loves the Father, and the Father loves Jesus. Their mutual love is a divine Person, God, the Spirit. The Spirit is Love at its greatest and most powerful.

Reflection: the Holy Spirit in my life. When the Father and Jesus send me their Holy Spirit, I am caught up into the love, the Love, between them. And I am empowered by the Spirit in my prayer and in my life — empowered to love and to receive love: with respect to Jesus and the Father, and with respect to the people in my life.

When I was baptized, I received the Holy Spirit. And as long as I am in a state of grace, in a right relationship with the Lord, then the Holy Spirit dwells in me, uniting me in a special way, through the Love that he is, to Jesus and to the Father.

But I can receive new and especially powerful outpourings of the Spirit. This is what the pentecostal churches and the charismatic renewal movements mean when they speak of a "baptism in the Holy Spirit." They mean a great and transforming pouring-out of the Spirit, a very great grace.

During your prayer time. Now, at this point in my retreat, I can enter into the mystery of Jesus' baptism in the Holy Spirit, and ask Jesus and the Father for a new outpouring of their Spirit. Pray with faith. You might want to begin by praying to Mary.

Prayer for a new outpouring of the Holy Spirit. Mary, my mother, pray with me now, and pray for me, to Jesus for a new outpouring of the Holy Spirit. I do want to receive, in a new and powerful way, now, the Spirit of Jesus and the Father. Help me to pray, and to open my heart.

God my Father, I come to you in and with and through your Son Jesus. And I ask you to send me your Holy Spirit of Love. Thank you, Father. Amen.

> *Other scripture texts*: Romans 8;
> John 3:1-10.

3. *Jesus heals me*

Place. The grounds around the church and the parish house. Almost always you can find pilgrims around the grounds of the parish church of St. James and the parish house. Often, especially during the late spring, summer, and early fall, great crowds assemble. The church, quite large for a parish church, nevertheless often cannot hold all the people who come for the evening rosary and the Mass. They spill over outside the church. Frequently even the special wooden benches set up outside cannot accommodate everyone.

People come in such large numbers because they believe that the mother of Jesus has specially chosen that place and that parish and that church, that she has visited it in a special way, and that her special presence continues there. And where Mary is in a special way, so is Jesus. So people come, looking for God, looking for the Lord. They did the same during Jesus' lifetime here on earth. They came looking for God and looking for healing.

Crowds around the church and the parish house

Sometimes the crowding at Medjugorje can become intense. When Our Lady appeared daily in the auxiliary sacristy in the church, and later when she appeared in a room in the parish house, often crowds struggled to get into the sacristy or the room to be present when Mary came to the young people. It could be hectic. Even now the crowding into the parish church in the evening can get oppressive.

And yet, with all the crowds and the crowding, perhaps partly because of that and partly because all have come for the same purposes, you can find at Medjugorje a wonderful spirit of helpfulness, of cooperation, of love — among the milling crowds of foreigners, Croatians, and villagers; and in the homes where most pilgrims stay.

You do not know everyone. You may know no one. But you do know that you are together with everyone in the Lord.

The healings that take place at Medjugorje are signs of the presence of the power of God. They increase our faith. And they show the quality of the Lord's love; compassionate and forgiving and healing.

Message from Our Lady

These days people from all nations will be coming to the parish. And now I am calling you to love. First of all love your own household, and then you will be able to accept and love all who come.

(June 6, 1985)

Scripture text

So many people came together as to have no room for them all, even at the door of the house, and he preached the word to them. Four men came carrying a paralytic to him. And, unable to bring the man in because of the crowd, they made a hole in the roof above Jesus and lowered through it the mattress with the paralytic on it. Seeing their faith, Jesus said to the paralyzed man, "Child, your sins are forgiven." Some scribes and pharisees were sitting there thinking in their hearts, "Why does this man speak like that? He blasphemes. Who except God can forgive sins?" Understanding their thoughts in his own mind, Jesus said to them, "Why do you think these things in your hearts? Which is easier to say to the paralytic, 'Your sins are forgiven,' or 'Pick up your mattress and walk'? But so that you may know that the Son of Man has authority on earth to forgive sins" — and then he said to the paralytic — "To you I say: get up, pick up your mattress, and go home." Right there the man got up, picked up his mattress, and in front of everyone walked out (Mark 2:2-12).

During your time of prayer. Imagine the crowd in and around the church of St. James at Medjugorje in the evening, like the crowd in and around the house trying to get in to Jesus. Jesus picks you out of the crowd and says to you, "Child, your sins are forgiven." How do you react? What do you say to Jesus?

He is here with you now. Tell him what is in your heart. Close this book now, and be with him quietly.

Some points for further prayerful reflection

(1) Each one of us is the paralytic. And each of us is one of the people who helped him by removing the roof tiles to make a hole and by letting the paralyzed man down into the presence of Jesus.

Lord Jesus, help me help others to you. And to let others help me to you.

(2) Jesus forgives you. And he wants to heal you. To heal whatever in you might in any way block your closer union with him. He wants to heal the fears that tend to paralyze you, the

anger and resentment that paralyze your love, the depression that takes away your hope and leaves you motionless and unable to step ahead. He wants to fill you with forgiveness and to take away the guilt feelings that oppress you and keep you down.

Heal me, Jesus.

(3) Let Jesus teach you his gentleness and compassion, and his love for you that heals you and makes you whole.

Thank you, Jesus, for loving me tenderly and with forgiveness.

4.   *Jesus is Lord*

Place. The hill of Podbrdo. Sit there with Our Lady, looking out over the plain, the fields and villages, the church, the distant mountains, and Mount Krizevac, surmounted by the cross of Jesus.

Message from Our Lady

Open your hearts to the Lord of all hearts.
(June 20, 1985)

61

Scripture text

In a discussion with the Jewish teachers
and leaders, Jesus asks them a question:
"What is your opinion about the Messiah?
Whose son is he?" "David's," they told him.
"Then how is it" he said "that David,
moved by the Spirit, calls him Lord, where
he says, 'The Lord said to my Lord: Sit at
my right hand, and I will put your enemies
under your feet'? If David can call him
Lord, how can he [the Messiah] be David's
descendant?" (Matthew 22:42-45).

Prayer for the grace I want. Lord Jesus, you
are Lord of all things. I ask the grace, Jesus, to
take you as Lord of my entire life, in all its
aspects. ˋ

Reflection: Jesus is Lord. Jesus asks them a
question they cannot answer. How can David,
who should be greater than the Messiah, call
the Messiah "Lord" when he writes at the beginning of Psalm 110 "The Lord [God] said to my
Lord [the Messiah] . . ." (verse 1)? The answer is
that the Messiah is divine, God, and therefore
Lord even in the sense that God is Lord. But the
leaders and teachers, even if they figured that
out, did not want to go into the question.

Peter, in the first Christian sermon at

Pentecost, under the inspiration of the Holy Spirit, quotes Psalm 110 in calling Jesus "Lord": "The whole house of Israel can be certain that God has made this Jesus whom you crucified both Lord and Christ" (Acts 2:36). From that moment on, "Lord" is the name most frequently given to Jesus.

In the Old Testament, only God is truly Lord: "Lord" means "God." The early Christians call Jesus "Lord" because they want to profess him as God, and equal to and "sitting at the right hand" (Psalm 110) of the Father. And so "Jesus is Lord" becomes the slogan of the early Christians and a common phrase in the New Testament.

The Letter to the Philippians speaks of the name that Jesus has as "above every other name, so that everything in heaven, on earth, and under the earth should bend the knee at the name Jesus has, and every tongue acclaim that Jesus Christ is Lord" (Philippians 2:9-11). The *name* in that text is not "Jesus" but "Lord." "Lord" is the name, the title, above all other names and titles.

That Jesus is Lord means not just that he holds an important title, like "king" or "president," and not just that he has the supreme authority. The letters of Paul to the Ephesians (chapters 1, 2 and 3) and Colossians (chapters 1 and 2) show what Jesus' lordship really means.

Jesus "holds all things in unity"; he holds everything together (Colossians 1:17), in existence. Jesus "is the ruler of everything, the head of the Church, which is his body," and "he fills all of creation" (Ephesians 1:23). Jesus, then, is Lord in the sense that he holds everything together and that he fills all things with his presence.

The Father's plan for the world is this: to "bring everything together under Christ as head, everything in heaven and everything on earth" (Ephesians 1:10), so that "all things be reconciled through him and for him" (Colossians 1:20). What is more, God's plan for the world, to bring everything into a unity in Jesus, is also God's plan for each of us. The world can find its true fulfillment only in Jesus Christ. So too for each of us: "In him you too find your own fulfillment" (Colossians 2:9).

Reflection: Jesus is my Lord. The Lord of the whole universe is also my personal Lord, the Lord of me, of the person I am. He knows my name. He knows everything about me, good and bad, past and present and future. He accepts me completely and unconditionally. And he calls me by name. He calls me to take him as the Lord of my life.

Of my whole life. Nothing in my life holds no interest for Jesus. He takes interest in all my relationships, in my health, in my money problems, in what I do every day, in how I feel, in what I think, in my fears and sadnesses and resentments, in my joys and thrills and happy surprises. And he wants to be Lord of all that, of everything in my life.

I can bring things under Jesus' lordship. My relationships: with each person I love, with each person I have problems with or a difficult relationship with, with each member of my family, with the people I see every day. With people in my past who have hurt me, with those whom I have hurt, with people who have helped me.

My health, my weight problem, my nervousness or sleeplessness. My need for inner healing.

My temptations and sinful tendencies. My weaknesses. My fears. My worries about the future.

My financial problems. The choices I have to make. My mistakes.

Everything to Jesus, into his hands, under his lordship. I want him to be Lord of everything in my life.

Reflection: distractions. When I pray, any real distractions I might have can give me clues as to what I still need to give over to Jesus, to put under his lordship. For example, if the thought of someone I love distracts me, I have a signal that that relationship stands to some extent out-side my relationship with Jesus. It contains an element or some elements that lead me away from Jesus — in the form of a distraction in my prayer, and so too somehow in my life outside my prayer. Perhaps some selfishness in my love, some possessiveness, some failure to love with an open hand.

What can I do? I can make the content of my distraction the content of my prayer; I can pray about the distraction. I lift that person up to Jesus. I put the relationship completely un-der the lordship of Jesus. I ask the Lord to purify my love of selfishness and of possessive-ness, to help me to love the person as a subject and not at all as an object. Doing that, I get more of my life under Jesus' lordship.

Again, the thought of someone who has hurt me might distract me in my prayer. This shows me that that relationship, and the hurt I have received, have not sufficiently come under the lordship of Jesus.

Right there, in my prayer, I can bring the hurt and the whole relationship to Jesus, under his lordship. I can forgive the person who hurt me, pray for that person, and hand the entire situation over to the Lord. When I do, I coop-erate with God's plan to bring everything in my life together under one head, Jesus. I center myself and my life more under the Lord with the help of his grace.

I can do the same with any distraction when I become aware of it as a distraction. In that way, I will help Jesus to integrate everything in my life around my relationship with him. He will become more the Lord of my life.

Prayer. Lord Jesus, I take you as Lord of my life, of my whole life. Of everything in my life. And of myself. I give myself wholeheartedly to you, without any reserves. I give you my heart. Jesus, be the Lord of my life. Thank you Jesus, because you are the Lord of my life. Amen.

> *Scripture texts if you need them*:
> Philippians 2:9-11; Colossians 2:9;
> Ephesians 1:3-12; Psalm 139: 1-17.

5. *The Eucharist*

Place. Before the Blessed Sacrament. There is eucharistic adoration each Thursday evening at Medjugorje, and each Saturday the young people who are in the prayer groups spend the night in adoration.

Message from Our Lady

> Adore continually the Most Holy Sacrament. I am always present when the faithful are in adoration. Special graces are then being received (March 15, 1984).

Scripture text

> Jesus said: "I am the bread of life; he who comes to me shall not hunger, and he who believes in me shall never thirst. . . . All that the Father gives me will come to me; and he who comes to me I will not cast out" (John 6:35; 37).

Prayer for the grace I want. Jesus, you are the bread of life. Help me to know you better, so that I can love you more and follow you more closely.

Reflection: Jesus in the Eucharist. We come to Jesus, to receive life, to receive all our hearts hunger and thirst for. What power comes from the presence of Jesus, God and Man! If we were to be in the same room as radioactive material, we would be affected for life. Here, on the altar, we have all the power and glory of God, beneficently irradiating us.

The presence of the Lord . . . the glory of his might (2 Thessalonians 1:9).

During your prayer time. For this retreat exercise, it is suggested that, if possible and not inconvenient, an hour be spent before the Blessed Sacrament, with faith in the reality of Jesus' presence.

Prayer is receiving, more than doing. Stay with Jesus, mostly silently, loving, receiving. Praise him with the angels who surround his glory. See what Our Lady is doing, and be with her. You could sing a hymn from time to time. Pray the way Jesus leads you.

Scripture texts to use if you need them.
John 6:51-58; John 18:24-26.

P A R T   IV

The Passion and Death of Jesus: The Sorrowful Mysteries and the Stations of the Cross

Note on fasting. At Medjugorje Our Lady has often recommended the traditional Christian practice of fasting. Most people in the parish fast on Wednesdays and Fridays, each as he or she can. Many fast on bread and water.

You may feel led by the Lord to fast especially during this fifth part of the retreat. If you are making your retreat in everyday life, then you might want to fast in some way (skipping a meal, skipping desserts, or any other way to fast you might feel called to), especially on Wednesday and Friday.

But fasting is a gift. If and when you fast, ask the Lord for the grace to fast, for the *gift* of fasting.

1. *Jesus' agony in the garden*

Place. On Mount Krizevac, by the cross, at night or in the very early morning.

Message from Our Lady

I especially ask you to venerate the heart of my Son. Make atonement for the wounds inflicted on the heart of my Son. That heart has been offended with all sorts of sin (April 5, 1984).

Scripture text

Then he left to go, as he usually did, to the mountain of the olives; his disciples followed him. When he arrived at that place he said to them, "Pray so as not to enter into temptation." He withdrew about a stone's throw, and kneeling down prayed, "Father, if you will, take this cup away from me; but not my will but yours be done."

An angel from heaven appeared to him and strengthened him. Going into an agony, he prayed more earnestly, and his sweat fell to the ground like drops of blood. Getting up from prayer and coming to the disciples, he found them sleeping, overcome with grief. And he said to them, "Why are you sleeping? Get up and pray lest you enter into temptation" (Luke 22:39-46).

Prayer for the grace I want. Lord Jesus, help me to know you better so that I may love you more and follow you more closely. Help me to enter into the mystery of your agony on the mountain of the olive grove. Let me share in your anguish, in your mental suffering, in your prayer to the Father. Bring me close to you in your agony in the garden of olives.

During your prayer time. In your imagination, place yourself either on Mount Krizevac or on the mountain of olives. Be with Jesus in his agony and in his prayer to the Father. Let Jesus draw you quietly into his heart and into the mystery of his prayer and his suffering in the garden of olives.

2. *Jesus is scourged*

Place. Almost any place outside the parish of St. James at Medjugorje. For example, in the nearby town of Citluk, a small town with one main street, one hotel, and one bus stop. Citluk represents "the world," the world that condemned Jesus to be scourged and crucified. You are, and a part of each of us is, part of that world. Jesus suffered and died so that you, and all of us, could be saved to eternal life — and be healed in this life.

Jesus is scourged so that you might be healed of whatever in you tends to separate you in any way from him.

Message from Our Lady

> Dear children, you know I promised you an oasis of peace here [at Medjugorje]. But you are not aware that around every oasis is a desert where Satan is lurking, and he wants to tempt each one of you. Dear children, only by prayer are you able to overcome every influence of Satan in your locality. I am with you, but I cannot take away your free will (August 7, 1986).

Scripture texts

> Pilate, resolving to satisfy the crowd, released Barabbas to them, and — having had Jesus scourged — handed him over to be crucified (Mark 15:15).

. . . by whose stripes you were healed.

(1 Peter 2:24)

. . . through his wounds you were healed.

(Isaiah 53:5)

Prayer for the grace I want. Ask Jesus to give you the grace to know him better, especially here in his being tied to a column and being scourged, so that you can grow in loving him, and so follow him better.

During your prayer time. Let Jesus lead you into the mystery of his being beaten with whips. Be there with Jesus. Let him draw you into his heart and into his memory of what happened.

3. *Jesus is crowned with thorns*

Place. Almost anywhere outside Medjugorje. For example, the small town of Citluk a few miles away, with the local police station and town government that have so often, supported by the regional and national police and governments, harassed, persecuted, and imprisoned persons associated closely with the events at Medjugorje. They make fun of Medjugorje and also of all religion, especially of Christianity.

Message from Our Lady

> Dear children, you are forgetting that I want sacrifices from you, to help you, and to banish Satan. Therefore I call you again to offer sacrifices, with a special reverence towards God (September 18, 1986).

Scripture text

> Then the governor's soldiers took Jesus into the great hall, and they all assembled there against him. They stripped him and put a purple cloak around him. They braided a crown of thorns and put it on his head, and a reed in his right hand. They genuflected in front of him and mocked at him saying, "Hail, king of the Jews." They spat on him, and they took the reed and hit him on the head with it (Matthew 27:27-30).

Prayer for the grace I want. Lord Jesus, I pay you reverence. I come to you reverently in reparation for the lack of reverence of the soldiers and of so many others down through the ages, including myself. I come to you humbly in reparation for the physical suffering and the insults and humiliations you have undergone for me. Help me to know you better, especially

here, beaten and suffering and humiliated, so
that I can know you better and follow you more
closely.

During your prayer time. Let Jesus take you
into his heart and into his memory of what
happened to him when he was crowned with
thorns and mocked. Let him draw you right
into what happened, into his suffering. If you
should be led to experience emotions or tears,
do not fight it; those tears and emotions will
unite you more closely to Jesus.

4. *The way of the cross: stations one through ten:*
   Jesus carries his cross

Begin to follow the way (or stations) of the
cross, going slowly. You may need several
prayer times.

Jesus is God, and therefore is eternal. His
passion, then, is not a thing of the past. You can
walk with him now as truly as if you were with
him on the day "he went out carrying his own
cross" (John 19:17). He will see you beside him.

Place. Mount Krizevac. "Krizevac" means
"cross." Ascend the steep, winding, rocky path,

pausing at each of the fourteen stations (stopping places), until you reach the great cross on the summit. Walk with Our Lady. Watch Jesus, listen, speak to him. He and his mother remember. . . . Any cross you have, carry it with Jesus.

Message from Our Lady

> You have a great and heavy cross. But do not be afraid to carry it. My Son is with you (April 5, 1985).

Prayer for the grace I want. I want to enter into the interior sufferings of Jesus, to know him as loving me in his passion.

Lord Jesus, I join my crosses, especially [name any cross in your life, especially the most humiliating], to your cross. You carried the sins of all ages. My sins are there, I see you carrying them. Jesus, may I come to know you more, on this journey, love you more, and repent sincerely. Mary, I ask you to show me now "the blessed fruit of your womb, Jesus," as he carried the cross for me.

I. *Jesus is condemned to death*

I watch Jesus as he stands before Pilate. He has already endured the agony in the garden;

he has been betrayed by his friend, arrested, dragged off, imprisoned overnight, tried on the testimony of false witnesses, scourged, and crowned with thorns. He is standing there, on trial for my sin. Pilate gives judgment:

> I did not find this man guilty of any of the charges against him (Luke 23:14).

No, Jesus, you are not guilty, but I am.

> Christ died once for sins; a righteous person for the unrighteous, that he might bring you to God (1 Peter 3:18).

Prayer:
> I love you Jesus my Love, above all things.
> I repent with my whole heart for having offended you.
> Grant that I may love you always;
> then do with me what you will.

Remain a while with Jesus at this station.

II.   *Jesus receives the cross*

I watch Jesus as, burdened with the cross, he begins the journey to Calvary.

The Lord has laid on him the sins of us all
(Isaiah 53:6).
Ours are the sufferings he bore, ours are
the sorrows he carried (Isaiah 53:4).
If you want to come after me, deny yourself and take up your cross daily and follow
me (cf. Luke 9:23).

Prayer:

I love you Jesus my love, above all things.
I repent with my whole heart for having
offended you.
Grant that I may love you always;
then do with me what you will.

III. *Jesus falls*

His distress is too great. The load he carries
crushes him as "he takes our infirmities and
bears our diseases" (cf. Matthew 8:17). This is
literally true. Jesus has compassion for me, suffers with and in place of me. Do I compassionate him, suffer with him, even in little ways, to
accompany him on this journey? I can join even
my falls to his — he understands, because "he
was tempted in all things as we are, though
without sin" (Hebrews 4:15). Watch Jesus:

It was the will of the Lord to wound him;
he has given him suffering (Isaiah 53:10).

Prayer:
>I love you Jesus my Love, above all things.
>I repent with my whole heart for having offended you.
>Grant that I may love you always;
>then do with me what you will.

IV. *Jesus meets his mother*

Stay close to Jesus and Mary at this stopping place, this station. Watch, listen. They have both come to this point for me. But also, Jesus is carrying his cross for his mother. She too had to be saved by his death. The redemption Jesus bought for us was applied to Mary at her conception, and she remained sinless. It was applied to me at my baptism. I can keep that salvation, or reject it by grave sin. Always, through the blood of Jesus, I can regain it. Speak with Mary; join with her gratitude for salvation. Compassionate her. Thirty years earlier when she joyfully carried the infant Jesus into the temple, the old man Simeon, who met them there, said to her: "A sword will pierce your soul" (Luke 2:35). It does so now as she meets her Son. Stay with her, she loves you.

Prayer:
>I love you Jesus, my Love, above all things.

81

I repent with my whole heart for having
   offended you.
Grant that I may love you always;
then do with me what you will.

V. *Simon helps Jesus to carry his cross*

I look on as they stop a passerby, Simon
from Cyrene, coming in from the country, the
father of Alexander and Rufus, and they make
him shoulder the cross and carry it behind Jesus
(cf. Mark 15:21 and Luke 23:26). Imagine Simon's feelings — his anger, resentment, burn-
ing shame. He is just going about his business,
hurting no one. What has he done to deserve
this? Why should he submit — he has not vol-
unteered to carry this cross; it has been inflicted
on him, and what will he get for it? Some things
he can accept, but not this. So it is often with my
crosses — the very thing that is most galling —
some other suffering, I think, I could manage,
but not this one. My inability to suffer "grace-
fully" or with dignity gives the cross that cutting
edge that defeats me. But it seems that Simon's
sharing in Jesus' sufferings, "filling up what is
lacking in Christ's affliction" (Colossians 2:24),
is rewarded by the grace of coming to know
Jesus, and not only for himself, but for his
family. St. Paul years later speaks affectionately

of Simon's wife and their son Rufus: "Greet Rufus, chosen in the Lord, and also his mother and mine" (Romans 16:13).

> Rejoice inasmuch as you share in Christ's sufferings, that you may also rejoice and be glad when his glory is revealed.
>
> (1 Peter 4:13)

At Medjugorje Our Lady said:

> These days, while we are joyfully celebrating the cross, I desire that your cross also is a joy for you. Especially, dear children, pray that you may be able to accept illness and suffering with love, as Jesus accepted them. Only in that way, with joy, shall I be able to give you the graces and healings which Jesus allows me (September 11, 1986).

Look at your reaction to the crosses in your life. Ask to see them from Jesus' point of view.

Prayer:
> I love you Jesus my Love, above all things.
> I repent with my whole heart for having offended you.
> Grant that I may love you always;
> then do with me what you will.

VI. *Veronica wipes Jesus' face*

"As long as you did it to the least of my brothers, you did it to me" (Matthew 25:40). So I *have* wiped Jesus' face. I have helped him on this way of the cross. I can be thankful now as I watch this encounter.

Veronica is not afraid to step out from the crowd — to be ridiculed by her neighbors, jostled by the ribald soldiers, roughly treated by officials. Many see what is happening but do not intervene (my sins of condoning injustice, through fear, self-protection, not wanting to get involved). What Veronica can do is little, but she does it. Jesus is still being crucified today: "Inasmuch as you have done it to . . . you have done it to me" (Matthew 25:40). What am I doing about social sin, institutional sin?

> If you do not speak to warn the wicked to renounce his ways, he shall die for his sin, but I will hold you responsible for his death. But if you warn the wicked to renounce his ways, and he does not, he will die for his sin, but you yourself will have saved your life (Ezekiel 33:8-9).

Do I reach out to even the most unattractive? Do I see Jesus in everyone?

The crowds were aghast when they saw
him; he looked so disfigured that he
seemed not human (Isaiah 52:14).

Once he was "the fairest of the sons of men"
(Psalm 45:2); now he "has no beauty or grace
that we should look at him, and no majesty to
attract us. He is despised and rejected by men, a
man of sorrows and acquainted with grief, one
from whom people shield their faces" (cf. Isaiah
53:2). "As long as you did it to the least, you did
it to me" (Matthew 25:40).

Prayer:

I love you Jesus my Love, above all things.
I repent with my whole heart for having
    offended you.
Grant that I may love you always;
then do with me what you will.

VII. *Jesus falls again*

I am poured out like water,
and all my bones are out of joint. . . .
You have laid me in the dust of death.
                        (Psalm 22:14-15)

Jesus is here in place of sinners — sinners
"in the dust of death," unable to cut sin out of

their lives, unable to change. Our Lady said she came to Medjugorje to call us to conversion:

> Dear children, again I invite you to prayer of the heart. If you pray in your heart, dear children, the ice-cold hearts of your brothers and sisters will melt, and every barrier will disappear. Conversion will be easily achieved by those who want it. You must intercede for the gift of conversion for your neighbor (January 23, 1986).

Seeing Jesus lying in the dust, hear him saying: "What I want is that they may be converted and live" (Ezekiel 33:11). Pray for the conversion of sinners; pray for graces of conversion for yourself.

Prayer:
> I love you Jesus my Love, above all things.
> I repent with my whole heart for having
>   offended you.
> Grant that I may love you always;
> then do with me what you will.

VIII.   *The women mourn for Jesus*

Jesus does not seem to accept the tears of these women. He speaks to them sadly, warning them that if suffering like his could befall the innocent, what will be the fate of the guilty? "If they do this when the tree is green, what will they do when it is dry?" (Luke 23:31). Jesus knew the devastation that was to come on Jerusalem: "Weep not for me, but for yourselves and your children" (Luke 23:28). The devastation threatening our world because of sin — abortion, nuclear arms, immorality, terrorism, torture, the oppression of peoples, the rejection of faith — is on a scale never known before. Our Lady says:

> Christians have forgotten that they can prevent war, and even natural calamities, by prayer and fasting (July 21, 1982).

Tears of compassion for suffering are useless unless they lead to action — to change of life. Jesus' mother says:

> I appeal to each one of you to make a conscious decision for God, and against Satan (May 25, 1987).

> Stand with the group of women, and ask yourself how effective your sorrow is.

Prayer:
I love you Jesus my Love, above all things.

I repent with my whole heart for having
    offended you.
Grant that I may love you always;
then do with me what you will.

IX. *Jesus falls a third time*

> Indeed we are weak in him, but we shall
> live with him by the power of God.
> (2 Corinthians 13:4)

Jesus knows my weakness that leads me to fall
back into sin. He knows that on my own I cannot make it. So he puts all the power he has as
God, at my disposal, saying to me: "My grace is
sufficient for you, for my power is made perfect
in weakness" (2 Corinthians 12:9).

Prostrate with Jesus, hand over to him any
particular weakness in your life, and receive the
power of his grace. He compassionates, suffers
with, our weakness, understands it:

> For he was crucified in weakness, but lives
> by the power of God (2 Corinthians 13:4).

Prayer:
I love you Jesus my Love, above all things.

I repent with my whole heart for having
   offended you.
Grant that I may love you always;
then do with me what you will.

X. *Jesus is stripped of his clothes*

   Right at the beginning of his life on earth,
Jesus stripped himself of his glory as God:

> Though he was in the form of God . . . , he
> emptied himself, taking the form of a
> servant, taking on human likeness.
>
> (Philippians 2:6-7)

Now, in his passion, he goes further:

> I am a worm and no man (Psalm 22:6).

There is no depth to which I can sink that Jesus
has not been there, and meets me there with
compassion and mercy. He will stop at nothing
to save me because he loves me, and wants to
take me with himself to our Father. The joy of
saving me keeps Jesus on this way of the cross:

> Jesus . . . for the joy set before him en-
> dured the cross, despising the shame.
>
> (Hebrews 12:2)

Prayer:

> I love you Jesus my Love, above all things.
> I repent with my whole heart for having
>   offended you.
> Grant that I may love you always;
> then do with me what you will.

5.   *The way of the cross: stations eleven through
                fourteen: The crucifixion*

XI.   *Jesus is nailed to the cross*

Keep close to Our Lady. She speaks to us:

> I, the Mother, love you all. And in any
> moment when it is difficult for you, do not
> be afraid. I love you all, even when you are
> far away from me and my Son. I ask you
> not to allow my heart to cry tears of blood
> because of the souls who are being lost in
> sin. Therefore, dear children, pray, pray,
> pray (May 24, 1984).

Look at the wounds in Jesus' hands and feet:

They shall look at him whom they pierced.
(John 19:39; Zechariah 12:10)

Know that:

By his wounds we are healed (Isaiah 53:5).

Prayer:
I love you Jesus my Love, above all things.
I repent with my whole heart for having
offended you.
Grant that I may love you always;
then do with me what you will.

XII. *Jesus dies*

Standing by the cross of Jesus were his
mother . . . and Mary Magdalene.
(John 19:25)

We are graced to be here. Most of Jesus' friends
ran away. Perhaps I have sometimes run away
from the cross, or even from Jesus, when I
chose myself rather than him. But now I am
back. I am watching Jesus die — watching the
Light of the world being extinguished by my
sin.

There was darkness over the whole land.
(Luke 23:44)

Jesus' soul, too, is in darkness. He can no longer find his Father. He cries out:

My God, my God, why have you abandoned me? (Matthew 27:46).

Our Father "did not spare his own Son, but gave him up for us all" (Romans 8:31-32). Truly, "you were bought with a price" (1 Corinthians 6:20).

At the foot of the cross, as Life dies, speak with him.

Prayer:
I love you Jesus my Love, above all things.
I repent with my whole heart for having
offended you.
Grant that I may love you always;
then do with me what you will.

XIII. *Jesus is taken down from the cross*

Mary takes her dead Son into her arms. This is what my salvation is costing her; yet when, before he dies, he gives me to her, she accepts me as her child. "Woman, behold your son," he says to her.

> Dear children, today I want to wrap my mantle around you and lead you along the road of conversion. Dear children, I ask you to offer up to the Lord your whole past, all the evil that has accumulated in your hearts. I want each one of you to be happy, but sin prevents this. That is why you must pray — and in prayer you will find a new way to happiness. Joy will reveal itself to your hearts and you will be joyful witnesses. That is what my Son and I are waiting for in each one of you (February 25, 1987).

Can I refuse her anything?

Prayer:
> I love you Jesus my Love, above all things.
> I repent with my whole heart for having
> offended you.
> Grant that I may love you always;
> then do with me what you will.

93

XIV. *Jesus is laid in the tomb*

Death could not hold him (Acts 2:24).
For love is strong as death
(Song of Songs 8:6).
Death was swallowed up in victory
(1 Corinthians 15:54).

The way of the cross at Medjugorje ends
not in the death of Jesus, but in the glorious
cross of victory over evil, which stands on the
summit overlooking all of Medjugorje — all of
the world. The inscription on it reads:

"Year 1933.
To the Redeemer of humanity, as a sign of
their belief and hope and love, Pastor
Bernardin Smoljan and the parish of Medjugorje have erected this cross. From every
evil deliver us, O Jesus."

Thanks be to God who gives us the victory
through our Lord Jesus Christ.
(1 Corinthians 15:57)

Thanks be to God who always leads us in
triumph in Christ, and through us spreads
everywhere the fragrance of the knowledge of him (2 Corinthians 2:14).

Ask at the foot of the cross for "the fragrance of the knowledge" of Jesus.

Prayer:
> I love you Jesus my Love, above all things.
> I repent with my whole heart for having
>   offended you.
> Grant that I may love you always;
> then do with me what you will.

Ivan, Jakov, and Marija see Our Lady

PART V

The Peace of Christ:
The Glorious Mysteries

Note on peace. Our Lady at the beginning of her daily visits to Medjugorje identified herself as the Queen of Peace. She applies that title to herself now in our times when there is so little peace in the world.

And she calls us to pray for peace: peace in the world, among peoples and nations; peace within nations among opposed parties and factions; peace in our own cities and towns and regions. And peace in our families; and peace in our hearts.

Peace begins at home, in my own heart. It begins and continues with my continuous conversion from sin and to Jesus, with my acceptance of his call and of the increase in faith that he offers me, and with my prayer and fasting.

This last part of the retreat is especially a time to open my heart to the peace he gives me. "Peace I bequeath to you. My own peace I give you. Not as the world gives, do I give to you. Do not let your heart be troubled or fearful" (John 14:27).

On March 24, 1988, Our Lady's message was:

> Dear children, again today I invite you to total abandonment to God. You are not aware, dear children, how great is the love with which God loves you. This is why he permits me to be with you, to instruct and help you on the way of peace. But you will not find this road if you do not pray. Therefore, dear children, put aside everything, and consecrate your time to God, and God will give you his gifts and will bless you. Do not forget, little children, that your life is passing, like a tiny spring flower which today is wonderful, but tomorrow nothing of it is left. For this reason, pray in such a way that your prayer and your abandonment to God point in that direction. That way your witness will be not only for yourself but for eternity.

1. *Jesus has risen*

Place. Imagine yourself present during the appearance of Our Lady. The glorious Queen of Peace, clothed in holiness, is living in the resurrection of her Son. She told the visionaries at Medjugorje to tell the people: "Believe as if you see." Believe that she is present to you now, though you do not see her. She draws you to Jesus.

Message from Our Lady

Open your hearts, and give your lives to

Jesus, so that he works through your hearts (May 23, 1985).

Scripture text

As they were speaking about him, he stood in their midst and he said to them, "Peace be with you." But they were frightened, terrified, and thought they saw a ghost. He said to them, "Why have you been troubled, and why are such ideas coming up in your minds? Look at my hands and feet and see that it is really me."
(Luke 24:36-39)

Prayer for the grace I want. Risen Lord Jesus, I ask the grace to know you better, so that I may love you more, and follow you more closely. Jesus, I rejoice in your resurrection. Now you come as consoler. Let me know you better. Teach me to pray.

Reflection: Jesus is risen. In Fra Angelico's frescoes of the resurrection, the bare feet of the risen Jesus walk over the spring grass as he comes from the tomb. Wherever his feet pass, little flowers spring up. The risen, beautiful Jesus is life-giving. He is Life.

"I am the resurrection and the life" (John 11:25). And he is with you now, in your prayer, raising you up, giving you life.

As you are before Jesus now, accept all his love for you — he loves you unconditionally, with his whole heart. He died for you, so what will he not do now that he is risen? Give him joy now by opening your heart, accepting all that love, and giving yourself over to him.

In his resurrection, Jesus is the consoler. His passion is over; my difficulties and sufferings continue. But, though there are times for crying out to the Lord in prayer because of my sufferings and sins, and those of others, there are times for putting my cares aside, and thinking only of him. Our Lady says:

> I have come to earth to teach you how to listen out of love, how to pray out of love, and not out of compulsion because of the cross you are carrying.
>
> (November 29, 1984)

Jesus risen is my hope, my future.

> He who raised up the Lord Jesus will raise us up also (2 Corinthians 4:14).

> For I know that my Redeemer is alive, and he, finally, will take his stand on earth. After my awakening he will set me close to

him, and from my flesh I shall look on God
(Job 19:25-27).

But my resurrection in Jesus risen is not
only for the next life. It begins now.

Set your minds on heavenly things, not on
the things on the earth, because *you have
died, and now the life you have is hidden with
Christ* in God. But when Christ is revealed,
and he *is* your life, you too will be revealed
in glory with him (Colossians 3:2-4).

During your prayer time. If I have any worries
or fears in my life, or for my future, I can put
them now into Jesus' hands. In my prayer now,
I know he is standing before me, saying:

Why are you troubled . . . See . . . it is I
myself (Luke 24:38-39).

Stay in your prayer with Jesus risen — your
life, your consoler, your future. Accept the
peace he gives you.

Scripture texts to use if you wish:
John 20;
John 11:23;
Romans 6:5-11.

2. *The Ascension*

Place. Podbrdo, the hill of the apparitions. From there one can look down onto the plain below: houses, fields, vineyards, the church. To your left is the higher hill, Krizevac, with its huge cross against the sky.

This cross on the hilltop has no figure of Christ on it. It is the cross of victory over all evil. It was erected in 1933, to celebrate nineteen hundred years of redemption. Our Lady told the visionaries that she prays daily at the foot of the cross. With her, we can appropriate and live in the redeemed life that Jesus won for us.

Message from Our Lady

I appeal to each one of you to begin to live as from today, that life which God desires of you — and that you begin to perform good deeds with love and mercy. What I require from you, dear children, is that each one of you lives a new life without destroying everything God does within you and presents to you as a gift. I give you my special blessing and the assurance that I am always with you on the road to conversion (March 25, 1987).

Dear children, today I want to invite you all, each one of you, to decide for heaven.

The way is difficult for all those who have not decided for God (October 25, 1987).

Scripture text

Jesus said, "You will receive power when the Holy Spirit comes upon you, and you will be witnesses to me both in Jerusalem and in all Judea and Samaria and to the ends of the earth." Saying this, and as they looked on, he was taken up into a cloud and out of their sight (Acts 1:8-9).

Prayer for the grace I want. Jesus, I come into your presence now; you are alive, glorious, reigning as Lord of all things. Let me know you better, so that I may be entirely under your lordship.

Reflection: seeing things from Jesus' point of view. After Jesus had entered heaven, the apostles returned to Jerusalem to wait for the promised Holy Spirit, and then to get on with their lives, and to spread the good news. They did not stay on the hillside, their eyes fixed on heaven. How then can St. Paul write: "Set your minds on heavenly things, not on those that are on the earth" (Colossians 3:2)? Should we not be concerned with earthly things: our lives, the good of others? Yes, but we have to get our angle of vision right. We have to see everything from a heavenly view.

Our glory, which will be revealed at the final coming of Christ (cf. Colossians 3:4), is that we are like God, made in his image. We need to see ourselves from God's viewpoint — not as human persons with souls, but as spirit persons with bodies. Jesus says, "God is spirit" (John 4:24), and in the creation story God says, "Let us make man in our image" (Genesis 1:26). So, looking at ourselves from God's angle, we are spirits with bodies.

God saw our tendency to live the wrong way round, in the days of Noah, when, as the book of Genesis tells the story, he almost had to give up on mankind:

> My Spirit will not strive with man, for he is flesh (Genesis 6:3).

But God sent his only Son in the flesh, to teach us how to live, with due reverence for the body, but led by the spirit.

> Sending his own Son in the likeness of sinful flesh . . . he condemned sin in the flesh . . . in order that . . . [we] might . . . walk not according to the flesh, but according to the Spirit (Romans 8:3-4).

104

Jesus risen and ascended is filling us, soul and body, with his life. St. Paul prays that

> . . . the God of our Lord Jesus Christ, the Father of glory, may give you a spirit of wisdom and of revelation in the knowledge of him, having the eyes of your hearts enlightened, that you may know what is the hope to which he has called you, what are the riches of the glory of his inheritance in the saints, and what is the outstanding greatness of his power in us who believe, according to the working of his mighty strength which he accomplished in Christ when he raised him from the dead and seated him at his right hand in the heavenly places.
>
> (Ephesians 1:17-20)

In prayer, ask for an interior knowledge of Jesus, to see things as he sees them. Accept him as your life, hope and future. Be face to face with him as he reigns now in glory.

> We all, with our unveiled faces reflecting like mirrors the glory of the Lord, are being changed from glory to glory into his image; this is the work of the Lord who is Spirit.
>
> (2 Corinthians 3:18)

And Mary tells us:

> Dear children, I desire you to be the reflection of Jesus who enlightens this unfaithful world which is walking in darkness. Dear children, you are not called to darkness, you are called to light. Therefore live the light with your lives (June 5, 1986).

Reflection: continuing to follow Jesus. Coming to the end of a retreat can mean that I might lose some of the graces God has given me: they get crowded out by "the cares of the world and the delight in riches, and the desire for other things" (Mark 4:19). So I need, at this stage of the retreat, to make some decisions — not great, lofty, impossible plans, but practical resolutions based on what I know Jesus has been saying to me during this retreat.

What is God's plan for my life? What is his call, as far as I see it now? I need to listen and to reflect, and to write down what I feel the Lord is calling me to. Perhaps to a more disciplined and more faithful life of daily personal prayer. Perhaps to more love and giving and care in my family or at school or at work. Perhaps to renounce some attachment that leads me into sin.

Take this matter of retreat resolutions to the Lord. Take it up with him in your prayer. Write down what you think he is calling you to.

Then, over a period of a few days, go over what you have written, revising it if necessary, and asking the Lord in prayer that he confirm it in your heart.

Daily, and at each moment during the day, my task is to look for him in love, to follow him, not my own desires. This I should do, without strain, just in love, like a small child. If I walk in love, even though I may not feel loving, I will find myself being generous with Jesus, without struggle.

For God loves a cheerful giver.
(2 Corinthians 9:7)

It is said that the best way to obtain any virtue is to act as though you have it. So, daily I cooperate in Jesus' project of love in my life. Our Lady tells us:

Dear children, today I want to appeal to all of you to start living a new life — as from today! It is my desire, dear children, that you come to understand how God has chosen each one of you, so that he may be able to use you in his great plan for the salvation of mankind. It is beyond your comprehension how great your role is in God's designs. Therefore, you must pray, dear children, so that in so doing you may be

107

enabled to grasp what God plans to achieve through you. I am with you in order that God's plan may be brought about in all its fullness (January 25, 1987).

But it is not going to be easy:

Anybody who tries to live in devotion to Jesus Christ is sure to be attacked.
(2 Timothy 3:12)

Reflection: in Jesus, victory over evil. We have to engage in spiritual warfare. Satan is determined to destroy us; at the very least, to undermine our participation in God's plan for us, in our relationship to him and to others.

We are not contending against flesh and blood, but against the principalities, against the powers, . . . against the spirits of wickedness (Ephesians 6:12).

We have to take every care and precaution not to open any door to the devil.

Do not leave any room for the devil.
(Ephesians 4:27)

Our Lady tells us how to act:

Dear children, hate gives birth to divisions . . . I invite you to carry unity and peace always. Especially, dear children, act with love in the place where you live. Let your only tool always be love. With love turn everything to good that Satan wants to destroy and take to himself. Only in this way will you be completely mine, and I will be able to help you (July 31, 1986).

Each evening, I should look at my life, and see where love has been today. St. Paul speaks of this:

There will be a resurrection of both the just and the unjust. So I always take pains to have a clear conscience towards God and towards men (Acts 24:15-16).

Spiritual warfare is real; my choice of God or self — heaven or hell — is real. But I live without fear. Jesus did not die for the ideal "me," the good me. "He died for us when we were still sinners" (Romans 5:8). So if I am a sinner, he is calling me; I qualify.

If by the one offense death did reign, how much more will the abundance of grace and the gift of righteousness reign in life through Jesus Christ (Romans 5:17).

Jesus has *given* us the victory; we can reign

now in our life, with his victory over temptation and evil.

> Thanks be to God, who always leads us in Christ in triumph (2 Corinthians 2:14).

> You are God's, little children; . . . greater is the One in you than the one in the world.
> (1 John 4:4)

During your prayer time. Before Jesus, in my prayer now, I should look at his plan for my life; I should ask his help in deciding entirely and wholeheartedly for him, and in making those decisions for my daily life that I see are necessary in love. *I decide for him*, not for myself.

> How long will you go on limping with two different opinions? If the Lord is God, *follow him* (1 Kings 18:21).

I plan to live out my decision for Jesus.

> Be all the more zealous to confirm your calling and your election . . . so there will be abundantly provided for you entrance into the everlasting kingdom of the Lord and Savior Jesus Christ (2 Peter 1:10-11).

3. *Pentecost: receiving the Holy Spirit*

Place. The room where Our Lady appears. Mary was praying with the apostles in the upper room in Jerusalem on the day of Pentecost, when God the Holy Spirit descended upon them; "and they were all filled with the Holy Spirit" (Acts 2:4).

Message from Our Lady

> You do not know how many graces God is giving you . . . Ask the Holy Spirit to be poured on you (May 9, 1985).

> Pray that the Holy Spirit inspires you with the spirit of prayer; that you pray more (June 9, 1984).

Scripture text

> When the day of Pentecost had come, they were all gathered together, and suddenly there was a sound from heaven like a rushing of a violent wind, and it filled the whole house where they were sitting. And they saw tongues like fire on the head of each one. And they were all filled with the Holy Spirit and began to speak in unknown tongues as the Spirit led them (Acts 2:1-4).

Prayer for the grace I want. Lord Jesus, I ask you to send me your Holy Spirit. He is the Spirit of the knowledge of you. May he set my heart on fire with love of you. May he lead me to live for you, and to be your witness. I need your Holy Spirit, Jesus.

Reflection: a new outpouring of the Holy Spirit. When we were baptized we received God the Holy Spirit; the third Person of the Trinity came to live within us. How then can we ask for a new outpouring of the Holy Spirit? Because our capacity can be increased. "The Spirit is our life" (Galatians 5:26). We become more spiritually alive each time we receive a big grace — an outpouring of the Spirit. Our Blessed Lady was "full of grace," yet she was filled again at Pentecost. And the apostles on whom the Holy Spirit came down, received another infilling some days later. After Peter and John had been kept overnight in prison, they were released and joined the other apostles and disciples:

> When they were released they went to their friends . . . As they prayed, the place where they were assembled was shaken; and they were all filled with the Holy Spirit (Acts 4:23, 31).

Can everyone receive the Holy Spirit? God promised that it would be so:

I will pour out my Spirit on all mankind . . .
Even on the slaves will I pour out my Spirit
in those days (Joel 3:1).

We do not have to be "worthy." All we need to
do is believe. St. Paul wrote to the Galatians:

Was it because you observed the Law that
you received the Spirit, or because — hearing — you had faith? . . . Does God furnish
you the Spirit and work miracles among
you because you observe the Law, or because, hearing, you believed?
(Galatians 3:2-5)

We need to believe, and to desire:

Jesus shouted out: "If anyone thirsts,
come to me; and drink, whoever believes
in me . . ." He was speaking about the
Spirit which those who believed in him
were about to receive (John 7:37-39).

To believe and to thirst are two conditions,
and the third is to ask. The Holy Spirit is sometimes called the "Promise," because his coming
to us is the fulfillment of the promise God made
(see, for example, Joel 3:1), a promise repeated
by Jesus:

I shall ask the Father, and he will give you another Comforter to be with you for ever, the Spirit of truth whom the world can never receive since it neither sees him nor knows him; but you know him because he stays with you and is in you.

(John 14:16-17)

The Spirit, then, is sent by the Father, and by Jesus. Before he died Jesus said:

It is for your good that I go away; if I do not go away, the Comforter will not come to you; but if I go, I will send him to you (John 16:7).

What does the Holy Spirit do when he comes to me? He lives in me; I live by his life. He is Love in me. He is the knowledge of God in me. He prays in me. He is joy and peace in me. He teaches me. All his mighty power is at work in me.

The Spirit of God dwells in you.

(Romans 8:9)

Do you not know that you are God's temple and that God's Spirit makes his home in you? (1 Corinthians 3:16).

I am living by the life of God the Holy Spirit. So in my life I need to walk always with that Spirit. St. Paul urges us:

> If we live in the Spirit, let us also walk in the Spirit (Galatians 5:25).

And he describes how he does this:

> When I made my plans, did I make them lightly? Do I decide according to the flesh? . . . It is God himself who establishes us in Christ; he has anointed us, marking us with his seal and giving us his pledge of the Spirit in our hearts.
>
> (2 Corinthians 1:17, 21-22)

Walking in the Spirit, acting under his guidance, I walk in love. In the Trinity, the Father from all eternity looks at his Son with love. The Son looks at his Father in love. That mutual love is "empersoned" — is Love, the Holy Spirit, the third Person of the Trinity. Now:

> The love of God has been *poured* into our hearts by the Holy Spirit who has been given us (Romans 5:5).

All that love is available to me, poured out in my heart. St. John tells us that when God gives the Holy Spirit, he sends him generously:

God gives the Spirit without reserve.

(John 3:34)

St. Paul, writing to Titus, speaks of

> . . . the renewal in the Holy Spirit which he
> [the Father] *poured out upon us richly*
> through Jesus Christ our Savior.

(Titus 3:5-6)

Being the mutual love of the Father and
the Son, the Holy Spirit has perfect knowledge
of them. Living in me now, he discloses this
knowledge to me. Jesus promised:

> The Holy Spirit whom the Father will send
> in my name, will teach you all things.

(John 14:26)

The Spirit shows me the Father and Jesus:

> . . . the things that no eye has seen and that
> no ear has heard, things beyond the heart
> of man, all that God has prepared for
> those who love him. These God has re-
> vealed to us through the Spirit, for the
> Spirit reaches the depth of everything,
> even the depths of God (1 Corinthians
> 2:9-10).

In my seeking for Jesus, seeking to know him, I
have within me the Holy Spirit with his perfect
knowledge. His desire is to show Jesus to me:

> Call to me and I will answer you; I will tell
> you things beyond the reach of your
> knowledge (Jeremiah 33:3).

The Holy Spirit prays in me. I can unite
myself to that prayer. I can be always praying
when I realize that there is a constant spring of
prayer at the center of my being. Especially
when I think I cannot pray, I can advert to the
Spirit praying in me his ineffable prayer:

> The Spirit too comes to help us in our
> weakness. For we do not know what to
> pray for, but the Spirit prays for us with
> inexpressible groanings; and God, who
> searches our hearts, knows what the Spirit
> means (Romans 8:26-27).

To receive a new outpouring of the Holy
Spirit, I just need to ask Jesus and the Father to
send their Spirit. In prayer now, I can ask. God
takes each of us as we are, as he knows us in love.
He will send the Holy Spirit in great power, but
for some, that power will be gentle, for others it
will be like a mighty wind. For some the effect of
this prayer will be immediately felt, for others,
gradually. Ask in faith, with desire, and without
fear, trusting yourself to Love.

Scripture reading if needed.
Galatians 5:16-26.

4.   *The fourth and fifth glorious mysteries:*
      The Assumption of the Blessed Virgin Mary into
      Heaven, and the Crowning of Our Lady as
      Queen of Heaven

Place. Imagine yourself present when Mary appears in Medjugorje. She is just as present to you right now. And she is present, even though you cannot see her, body and soul.

How would she look and speak if you could see and hear her? Wherever she has appeared, Our Lady has always had the physical characteristics and the manner of the people in the place she visited: at Lourdes, like a country girl of that region, at Kibeko in Rwanda, Africa, black, and just like the people there; at Medjugorje, like a young Croatian girl of that area. And she always speaks not only the language of the place, but with the local accent. If you could see and hear her, you would find her astonishingly beautiful, but someone you could relate to easily.

Knowing that, even though you do not see or hear her, you can enter easily into a relationship with her now in your prayer. Ask her to pray with you, and to help you in your prayer.

Message from Our Lady

Dear children, today I will give you my

love. You do not know, dear children, how great my love is, and you do not know how to accept it. In different ways I wish to show it, but you, dear children, ask from God the graces he will grant through me. I am ready to obtain from God all that you ask, so that your sanctity may be complete. So it is, dear children, that you must not forget to ask, since God has promised to supply me with all the graces you need (August 25, 1987).

Scripture text

And a great sign was seen in heaven: a woman clothed with the sun, with the moon under her feet and a crown of twelve stars on her head (Revelation 12:1).

Prayer for the grace I want. Mary, my mother in heaven, whom Jesus took up to heaven to be with him bodily in glory, be with me now. Help me to pray. Pray with me and for me. Take me to Jesus.

Lord Jesus, I come to you with my mother and yours. Help me to know you better, to love you more, and to follow you more closely.

Reflection. The scripture text presents the Church in heaven, the New Jerusalem, under

119

the symbol of a woman clothed with the sun. But the Church, for example in the Mass of the Assumption, applies the text freely to Our Lady. And in the miraculous painting of Mary that resulted from her appearing to Juan Diego at Guadalupe in sixteenth-century Mexico, the Blessed Virgin does seem to be clothed with the sun; the moon lies under her feet, and she wears not a crown but a whole mantle covered with stars. The young people at Medjugorje do frequently see her with a crown of stars.

Mary, your mother, physically and gloriously present in heaven with the risen Jesus, and present to you now in your prayer, is truly your mother — the mother of your salvation, the mother of the Lord's grace in your life. Because she was and remains the mother of Jesus, and because Jesus came to us first through Mary, therefore — since that relationship, her motherhood of him, still holds — Jesus comes to us now always somehow through Mary. The Jesus-life in you, God's grace, comes through her. She is mediatrix of graces. Even though Jesus is your unique and only Mediator with the Father, still Mary, in another sense, is mediatrix of graces — all grace comes to you through her.

That does not mean you have to go to Mary for help. But it does mean that you *can*. She is your mother.

During your prayer time. Pray the way that seems the easiest and the most appropriate to you now. Go to Mary, and stay with her. Then with her go to Jesus. Or perhaps just stay with Mary. Or begin your prayer by going right to Jesus with Mary, and thank him for her in your life.

5.   *Final exercise: a contemplation for obtaining love*

Place. The place where Our Lady appears. See her before you, surrounded by heavenly light, accompanied by angels, as the visionaries often see her. With our mother, who is the Queen of Heaven, stand before God Our Lord, with the nine choirs of angels, and all our brothers and sisters, the saints. This is reality.

Message from Our Lady

> Dear children, I ask you to give thanks to God for all the graces that he gives you; give thanks to God for all the fruits of his grace, and praise him. Learn how to give thanks for little things, then you will be able to give thanks for great things (October 3, 1985).

Alleluia!

Give thanks to the Lord, for he is good,
   his love is everlasting!
Give thanks to the God of gods,
   his love is everlasting!
Give thanks to the Lord of lords,
   his love is everlasting!

He alone performs great wonders,
   his love is everlasting!
By wisdom he made the heavens,
   his love is everlasting!
He set the earth on the waters,
   his love is everlasting!

He made the great lights,
   his love is everlasting!
The sun to rule the day,
   his love is everlasting!
Moon and stars to rule the night,
   his love is everlasting! . . .

He led us through the wilderness,
   his love is everlasting! . . .

He remembered our lowliness,
   his love is everlasting! . . .
And saved us from our enemies,
   his love is everlasting!
He provides for all living creatures,
   his love is everlasting!

Give thanks to the God of Heaven,
  his love is everlasting!

(Psalm 136)

Prayer for the grace I want. Father, Jesus, Holy Spirit, I want to thank you for all your goodness to me. Thank you for the wonder of all reality. Open my eyes to see you working for me in everything. May I so know your love for me that I grow greatly in love for you.

Reflection. From all eternity God's love was for those whom he would make — and make in his own image. He furnished the universe and our planet, in beauty, for us:

> Thus heaven and earth were completed with all their array. And God saw everything that he had made, and indeed it was very good (Genesis 2:1 and 1:31).

And when we spurned his love, choosing self, God tried even more to convince us of his love, by the ultimate gesture of giving up his only, and beloved Son for us.

> God so loved the world that he sent his only Son (John 3:16).

And Jesus, the Son, gave his life for us. He said:

A man can have no greater love than to lay down his life for his friends. You are my friends (John 15:13).

Dying on the cross for me, Jesus is truly

> . . . the love of God made visible in Christ Jesus (Romans 8:39).

But how can God and a creature be friends? Our nature is wholly different. God and a creature — even that has been made possible, for God transformed our human nature, informed it, with a share of his divine life, so that we could be capable of friendship with him.

> What more could I have done for my vineyard that I have not done? (Isaiah 5:4).

I need to be convinced that at every moment of my life, sleeping and waking, God is loving me, is working for me in everything. In fact, my life comes from his hands moment by moment, breath by breath.

> All creatures depend on you. You turn away your face, they suffer; you stop their breath, they die (Psalm 104:27, 29).

In every flower, in every atom, God is working for me. In all things I can see the One who loves me.

You are Christ's and Christ is God's.
(1 Corinthians 3:22)

Even in my crosses, God is working for me.

How then can I not love him and give myself to him? Because even that comes as his gift — as a gift to be asked and sought after.

This then is what I pray, kneeling before the Father . . . Out of his infinite glory may he give you the power through his Holy Spirit for your hidden self to grow strong, so that Christ may live in your hearts, and then, planted on love, and built on love, you will with all the saints have strength to grasp the breadth and the length, the height and the depth, until knowing the love of Christ, which is beyond all knowledge, you are filled with the utter fullness of God (Ephesians 3:14-20).

During your prayer time. Remain before God. Let the angels and saints praise and thank him on your behalf. Sit in the sun of his love, absorbing the love of the Father, of Jesus, of the Holy Spirit. Ask for love and generosity.

Say this prayer slowly, perhaps several times:

Take, Lord, and accept all my freedom, my memory, my understanding, and my entire will, all that I have and possess. It is all yours, Lord. You gave it to me. I make it over to you. Dispose of it entirely according to your will. Give me your love and your grace, and I want no more.

Scripture readings if you need them.
Romans 8:28-39; Psalms 111 and 104.

Dear children, today I ask you to pray with your whole heart, and to change your life day by day. I especially ask you, dear children, to begin to live in a holy way, with prayers and sacrifices. Because I desire that every one of you who has been in this fountain, or near this fountain, of grace, will reach heaven by the special gift that has been given to me, that is, holiness.

Therefore, dear children, pray, and change your lives towards holiness. I shall always be close to you (November 13, 1986).

Pray; pray; pray! (a part of several messages).